BLACK UNITED METHODISTS

BLACK
UNITED METHODISTS

Retrospect and Prospect

by
J. H. Graham

*Board of Global
Ministries of the
United Methodist Church*

**African American Methodist Heritage Center
Madison, New Jersey**

BLACK UNITED METHODISTS
RETROSPECT AND PROSPECT

Copyright © 1979 by J. H. Graham, 2011 by James A. Graham

First published by Vantage Press, Inc.

This edition published by arrangement with Abingdon Press.

ISBN: 978-1-4267-4916-2

Manufactured in the United States of America

Dedicated to the
memory of
my dear wife, India Mae,
who taught me that
an event in
history must be
interpreted in the context
of yesterday and tomorrow.

Contents

CHAPTER

    Foreword
    Preface
    Acknowledgments

  I. Black People in Methodist Societies Prior to
       the Organization of the Methodist Episcopal
       Church, 1758–1783 1

  II. The Negro in the Methodist Episcopal
       Church Before the Schism, 1784–1844 16

  III. The Lull After the Storm, 1845–1863 26

  IV. The Period of Institutional Development,
       1864–1900 33

  V. Black Conferences Under White Leadership,
       1901–1919 73

  VI. Selected Black Conferences Under Black
       Leadership, 1920–1939 80

  VII. The Central Jurisdiction—The Price for
       Union, 1940–1974 91

  VIII. Special Honors and Distinguished Leadership
       Roles of Black Methodists in the Church and
       Society 108

  IX. Black United Methodists in Prospect 140
       Notes 157

Foreword

In the midst of ambiguities faced by The United Methodist Church as it attempted to live out its decision toward Black and white inclusiveness that eradicated the Central Jurisdiction, Dr. John H. Graham wrote this book, *Black United Methodists: Retrospect and Prospect.*

John Graham was one of a handful of African Americans serving on general boards of the church in the early 1970s. Like the others, John Graham represented the best of the minority race, serving as a committed pastor and scholar whose forté was as a research analyst and writer. Out of his own experience of a love-hate relationship with the Church, he used his skills to paint the progress toward inclusiveness in the Church, while sharing the ambivalence of the Church as it stumbled toward faithfulness.

For those desiring to read a concise but accurate historical outline of African Americans in The United Methodist Church, this is the book. For those desiring tidbits of data not included in typical history books, commingled with insertions of American history, this book will serve as a rich resource.

Graham's anecdotes include the initial caucus meetings of the Church, the unique personalities of General Conferences, the first African American bishops of The United Methodist Church, and a time line and description of the Central Jurisdiction.

The African American Methodist Heritage Center, created to assure that the rich history and personalities of African Americans are not lost, sees this book as a treasure in the venture of "telling our story."

As the philosopher and historian George Santayana once said, "Those who do not learn the lessons of history are doomed to repeat its mistakes." As the Church continues to strive toward total inclusiveness in many dimensions, we pray that this book, through the eyes and heart of John Graham, may be a profound teacher.

Bishop Forrest C. Stith
President, African American Methodist Heritage Center

Preface

This volume intends to portray the historical development of Methodism among black people since 1758. It traces in an abbreviated fashion the history of black Methodists through Methodist societies, the Methodist Episcopal church, the Methodist church, and the United Methodist church.

It describes in capsule form the development of annual conferences, institutions, and selected local churches. It enumerates the achievements of blacks in leadership roles within the church society.

This book provides an opportunity for contemporary black Methodists to become acquainted with their past. Understanding their Methodist heritage will enable them to understand themselves better. The late Dr. J. W. E. Bowen, Sr., said about six decades ago: "To understand the Negro today, one must study his past, for the fruitage of today was rooted in the past."

The last chapter, "Black United Methodists in Prospect," will make some suggestions for achieving *de facto* inclusiveness on the local church level. Will the black Methodists become a "leaven" or enclave?

This study is designed to be a descriptive study and not a normative study. The writer proposes to tell it as it was.

J. H. GRAHAM

Acknowledgments

It would be an impossible task to trace in details the provenence of every fact recorded in this volume. Many persons have contributed directly or indirectly to the writing of this book. I gladly acknowledge this honest debt, still not fully discharged.

Grateful acknowledgments are made to the Board of Global Ministries of the United Methodist Church for granting me a sabbatical leave in order that I could produce this book. I am grateful indeed to the publishers for written permission to use certain quotations. Special mention must be made of Dr. Robert Wilson of Duke University and Dr. W. T. Handy, Jr., of the United Methodist Publishing House for encouraging me to do this study.

Gratitude is in order for Dr. Robert Wilson and Mr. George Daniels of the Board of Global Ministries for their critical comments. I am indebted to Mrs. Anita Wilson for the preparation of the manuscript.

BLACK UNITED METHODISTS

CHAPTER I

Black People in Methodist Societies Prior to the Organization of the Methodist Episcopal Church, 1758–1783

Prior to the official organization of the Methodist Episcopal church in 1784, black people were followers of the Wesleyan movement. As early as 1758, black people were introduced to the Methodist movement. On November 29, 1758, John Wesley baptized his first Negro converts.

In his journal, Mr. Wesley records: "I rode to Wandsworth and baptized two Negroes belonging to Mr. Gilbert, a gentleman, lately from Antigua. One of these was deeply convinced of sin; the other is rejoicing in God her Savior and is the first African Christian I have known."[1] It was at Wandsworth, England, metropolitan borough of London, that black people became historically related to the Methodist movement.

These new converts soon became flaming evangels of the new truths. Their master, Nathaniel Gilbert, was influenced pervasively by them. He was converted to the Christian faith. By profession, he was a lawyer and planter. He served also as the speaker of the House in the islands. Shortly afterwards, he was a licensed local preacher in the Methodist movement.

1

These African Christians and their master are credited with having introduced the Methodist movement in the West Indies. According to Gregory, "the first Methodist chapel in the Torrid Zone was set up in Antigua, composed almost wholly of Negroes."[2] The home of Mr. Gilbert served as the first meeting place. By 1786, there were 1,569 members; only two were White.[3] By 1796, Dr. Coke reported that the West Indian Missions had increased to more than 10,000 Negro members.[4]

Early Black Evangelists

Once these early blacks were converted, they could not keep it to themselves. They became couriers of the good news. The shortest list of these early evangelists must include: Black Harry, Henry Evans, John Stewart, and Peter Williams.

The earliest of these black evangelists in the colonies was Harry Hoosier. He was called "Black Harry," for he was very black. The definition of Andrew Fuller of "black" could be appropriately applied to Black Harry—"image of God cut in Ebony." He was diminutive in stature but sun-crowned in character. He possessed great powers of persuasion. Although he was illiterate, he was indeed a gifted preacher. He was called, "The greatest orator in America," by Dr. Rush. Asbury alluded to him in 1780 as a suitable companion to preach to the colored people.

People came in crowds to hear Bishop Francis Asbury. On one occasion, the meeting house was too small to contain the people. Many had to hear from the outside. One eager listener spoke to another about the eloquence of the bishop. The man replied: "That's not the bishop but the bishop's servant." In amazement, the eager listener replied: "If such be the servant, what must the master be?" In alluding to Black Harry, Thomas Coke said: "I believe he is one of the best preachers in the world."

On September 11, 1786, Black Harry was permitted to

preach in John Street Church for the first time. The following comment was made later:

> Lately came to this city a very singular black man who is said to be quite ignorant of letters, yet he has preached in the Methodist Church several times to the acceptance of several well disposed judicious people. He delivers his discourses with great zeal and pathos and his language and communication is by no means contemptible. It is the wish of several of our correspondents that this same black man may be so far successful as to rouse the dormant zeal of members of our slothful white people who seem very little affected about the concerns of another world.[5]

Methodism reached the Dutch island of Saint Eustatius through the preaching of Black Harry, a Methodist slave from the United States. He preached with great power. The governor of the island attended the services and gave him every encouragement. Planters opposed the new movement. He was forbidden to preach or to hold any kind of public meeting. He continued to meet classes privately. Finally, he was beaten severely and sold out of the island.

Black Harry was very acceptable to other denominations as well. The Quakers believed that since he was unlearned, he preached by immediate inspiration.

It is conjectured that Black Harry died in 1806. In appreciation for his ministry, a large number of whites and blacks followed his body to its final resting place in Kensington, Pennsylvania.

The second black Evangelist possessed not only the gift of dynamic preaching but was a genius in church organization. In this regard, special mention must be made of Henry Evans. Unlike Harry Hoosier, Henry was a free-born Negro from Virginia. By trade, he was a cobbler. After his conversion, he became an itinerant local preacher. He organized the Fourth Street Church in Wilmington, Delaware. He continued southward along the Atlantic seacoast to Charleston, South

Carolina. En route, he stopped at Fayetteville, North Carolina. While there, he attended services of worship at Duggs Chapel. He introduced himself as a Methodist local preacher. Upon invitation of some of the white citizens, he consented to preach to their slaves. Very soon his preaching became an incipient threat to the status quo. What was said to Paul and Silas in Acts 17:6, "These men who have made trouble all over the world have come now here and Jason has harboured them," could very appropriately be applied to Henry Evans. The town council soon issued a ban on his preaching in Fayetteville. He had become indeed the eighteenth century troublemaker in this little quiet town.

Henry was forced outside the city limits, but the people followed him. Very soon the people had begun to exert social pressure on the town council to rescind its action. It soon prevailed, and Henry Evans was allowed again to return to Fayetteville and preach the uncompromising gospel.

Very shortly his genius of organization came to fruition. He organized a church here in 1790. It was named Evans Chapel in his honor. Both blacks and whites became members of this church. It became an early inclusive fellowship on the east coast of North Carolina. Abel Stevens said: "Henry Evans was confessedly the father of the Methodist church, white and black, in Fayetteville."[6]

The attendance of the whites and blacks continued to increase. Soon the blacks were crowded out of the church. Sheds were built on either side of the church to accommodate the black worshippers.

In speaking of his effectiveness, Joseph Travis, presiding elder of the Pee Wee District of the South Carolina Conference, remarked:

> He began more and more to elicit the attention of the white population. Ultimately, a white married lady of good mind and accomplished manners—a celebrated school mistress—joined the Methodist Episcopal Church . . . prejudice . . . began to melt like wax before the flame.

Other white citizens presented themselves for admission. His congregation became larger and respectable . . . he . . . transferred church, congregation and all over to the white preachers.[7]

In 1810, Evans Chapel Church was transferred to the South Carolina Conference upon the urgent request of its founder.

In 1810, Henry Evans died in Fayetteville. His last conscious act was to quote from I Corinthians 15:57: "But thanks be to God which giveth us the victory through our Lord Jesus Christ."

His funeral was preached by William Capers. He was buried under the chancel of the church that he had built.

At his death, the church was still flourishing. It had 110 white members and 87 Negro members. By 1817, Evans Chapel had a church membership of 520 members, 153 whites and 367 blacks.[8]

Peter Williams was also an early black lay evangelist. He was born on Beekman Street, New York City, of slave parents. He was described as of "pure African descent." He was a member of a large family—seven sisters and two brothers.

He married Mary Dunham, a native of Saint Christopher in the West Indies. Molly, as she was affectionately called, was the caretaker of the Methodist parsonage. She was already a member of John Street Society.

Soon after John Street Church was organized, he began to attend worship services there frequently. In 1768, he was converted under the preaching of Thomas Webb. He united with the John Street Society.

He was owned by James Aymor.[9] His master was engaged in the tobacco industry. His master was also a loyalist. After the Revolutionary War was over, Mr. Aymor decided to return to England. Peter persuaded his master to sell him to John Street Church. He was sold for forty pounds. This transferral of ownership was consummated on June 10, 1783. Immediately, Peter began to negotiate with the trustees for his freedom. His initial payment was with his own watch. The record shows that the church received at sundry times four pounds from Black Peter. Finally this entry: "By cash received of Peter Williams in full of all demands on the fourth day of November, 1785, five pounds seven shillings." Within twenty-nine months, Peter had bought his freedom.

He died in 1823. Coke, Asbury, Whatcoat and John Dickens paid tribute to his worth as a man and to his sterling Christian character.

The first home missionary in the Methodist Episcopal Church was John Stewart. He was a freeborn mulatto and was born in Powhatan County, Virginia.[10] After he reached the age of twenty-one, he developed wanderlust. He set out for Ohio. En route, he was robbed of his worldly possessions. After this experience in a strange land, Stewart began immediately to muse upon the condition of his soul. His parents were members of the Baptist church, but John was described as a "careless sinner."

In his sojourn, he stopped with a tavern keeper. This fact was conducive to the development of drug addiction. Very soon he had developed into an alcoholic, but one with a guilty conscience. He made frequent resolutions but found himself too weak to keep his resolutions.

His guilt was compounded by the death of a very intimate friend. The loss of his personal belongings, the distance from his family, the idea of poverty and disgrace, together with the wretched situation of his soul, drove him to the brink of despair. Several times he thought of committing suicide. One night, on his way to the river to drown himself, he was attracted by hymn singing in the distance. As he drew nearer, it became more inspiring. When he got to the house, he discovered that it was a Methodist prayer meeting.

His denominational prejudice against the Methodist denomination would not allow him to enter the meeting house at first. Curiosity prompted him. After long hesitation, he reluctantly entered. To his happy surprise, he found a cordial reception from a group of concerned Christians. Here he was encouraged to seek with all his heart the "last blessing." His deep-rooted prejudice began to melt slowly. According to Joseph Mitchell, it was then that he united himself with the people whom he formerly held in the greatest contempt—and "took their people to be his people, and their God to be His God."

Later, he attended a camp meeting conducted by the Reverend Marcus Lindsey. Very soon he was on the mourner's bench. Here he stayed all night in pursuit of the "last blessing." At daybreak, new light broke into his heart. He was converted to the Christian faith.

It was his ardent desire to grow in grace. Hence, he developed the practice of regular evening private devotions. One evening, a voice spoke to him in crystal clear language: "Thou shalt declare my counsel faithfully."

Like Moses, Stewart tried to conjure reasons for his refusing to preach. First, he felt unworthy of the call. He was not qualified for the sacred task. Like Jonah, he had an impulse to flee to Tennessee with friends. He was stricken with a severe illness. While bedridden, he promised God that if he recovered, he would become His gospel gleeman.

When he recovered, he kept his promise. Without bread or credentials, he crossed the Muskingum River by faith. He encountered sundry persons who strove in vain to dissuade him from his pursuit.

However, he met some friendly enemies on the other side of the river. They introduced him to the tribe of Delawares on the upper Sandusky River.

His first congregation consisted of two persons; an old Indian man named "Big Tree" and an aged Indian woman named Mary. They heard his message gladly.

Early, Stewart was confronted with a language barrier. Through the counsel of Mr. William Walker, the subagent amongst the Indians, he was directed to Jonathan Pointer. Jonathan Pointer was a black man. He had been taken prisoner by the Wyandotte Indians during his youth. He had learned to speak the native tongue of the Indians fluently.

On arriving at Mr. Pointer's home, Stewart introduced himself and his mission. Pointer was not too interested in his message. He also warned Stewart that others had made futile attempts. Besides, Pointer was making ready to attend a tribal feast and dance. Stewart asked leave to accompany him to the festivity. After much hesitation, Pointer reluctantly consented.

The tribal dance was indeed a festive occasion. At the close of the dance, Stewart asked permission to speak to the Wyandotte Assembly. At the end of his message, he requested that if they entertained feelings of friendship, to so signify by extending to him their right hand. The tribal chief—Two Logs, sometimes called Bloody Eyes—rose immediately and advised the group that they were duty bound to manifest their friendship to the stranger. Following the chief, the people extended their right hand to Stewart. Stewart announced then that he would preach at Mr. Pointer's home and invited the people to come.

In November, 1816, Stewart began his formal ministry to the Wyandotte Indians. His first convert was Big Tree. Later, four other tribal leaders were converted to the Christian faith—Between the Log, Monocue, Hicks and Peacock. Two converts became local preachers, Between the Log and Monocue.

Stewart had some success, but he had also many adversaries. Opposition to his ministry came from some white traders in the Wyandotte territory. They became suspicious of Stewart. They believed that he was an impostor and a runaway slave. They tried to persuade the Indians to drive him out of their territory. On hearing of this, Stewart went again to Mr. Walker for counsel. He was assured by the subagent to have no fear but continue to preach the gospel faithfully.

The Roman Catholic Church soon became his formidable foe. The priests accused Stewart of preaching a doctrine contrary to the Roman Catholic Church. A trial was demanded. Mr. Walker served as the judge. He examined Stewart's Bible and hymnal as well as the Catholic Bible. The decision of the judge was that Stewart's Bible was written in English and the Catholic version was Latin. He ruled further that Stewart's hymnal contained songs based on subjects from the Bible. Therefore, Stewart's Bible and hymnal were genuine and good.

John Stewart also had his "Mars Hill Experience." He challenged the old system of heathenism that was practiced in the territory. Two chiefs defended the customs. John Hicks spoke as follows:

> My friend, as you have given liberty to any one who had objections to the doctrines you teach and endeavor to maintain, to speak on the subject, and state their objections; I, for one, feel myself called upon to rise in defense of the religion of my fathers; a system of religion the great Spirit has given his Red children as their guide and the rule of their faith, and we are not going to abandon it so soon as you may wish; we are contented with it because it suits our conditions and is adapted to our capacities.[11]

Another defender of the faith was Monocue, the local preacher. Said he:

> I do not doubt but what you state faithfully what your book says; but let me correct an error into which you appear to have run and that is your belief that the Great Spirit designed that his Red children should be instructed out of it. This is a mistake. The Great Spirit never designed this to be the case.[12]

Stewart used the Bible in defense of his argument. He interpreted Matthew 28:19-20. He then said to them:

> You certainly consider yourselves a nation composed of human beings; if so, then you may rest assured that the gospel will be preached, not only to you but to all nations of the Indians.

The last objection raised against Stewart was that he was a preacher without credentials. Again, Judge Walker was asked to rule. It was the ruling of the judge that no law had been violated unless Stewart performs the rites of matrimony or baptism. "Any man has right," said the judge, "to talk about his religion and try to get others to embrace it."

Very soon afterwards, John Stewart went to Urbana, Ohio to attend a quarterly conference of the Mad River Circuit.[13] Some of his red converts accompanied him and recommended him for local license. In March 1819, Stewart was granted local license by the Mad River Circuit. According to Moses Crane, the presiding elder of the Miami District, the license was granted almost unanimously.

The Wyandotte Mission continued to grow. In 1822, Bishop William McKendree visited the mission. He found the mission in prosperous condition; it had a membership of 200.[14]

During the late summer of 1823, Stewart's health began to fail rapidly. On September 17, 1823, he called his wife to his bedside and articulated faintly these words: "Wife, be faithful." He died at high noon on Steptember 17, 1823 at the age of thirty-seven.[15] He was in his seventh year in the ministry of his Lord. He was buried in the center of the Indian reservation on the upper Sandusky.

The Beginnings of Methodist Societies in the United States

Just where Methodism began its first society was for a long time a moot question. Two churches ranked the same in priority. They were the Log Meeting House on Sam's Creek, Frederick County, and the John Street Church, New York City.

A joint commission composed of representatives of the Methodist Episcopal Church, the Methodist Episcopal Church South and the Methodist Protestant Church was appointed to settle this historic question. After a careful survey and examination of all available data, the commission concluded that priority should be given to the Log Meeting House on Sam's Creek.[16]

The Log Meeting House In Maryland

In 1764, Robert Strawbridge organized the first Methodist Society in America on Sam's Creek, Frederick County, Maryland. On his tombstone in Mount Olivet Cemetery, Baltimore, Maryland, the following words are inscribed: "He built the Log Meeting House in Frederick County, Maryland, 1764, the first in America."[17]

There were Negro members among the charter members of the first Methodist Society. The first records show that Aunt Sweitzer, a slave named Anne, was on the first class roll.[18] She was a slave of the Sweitzer family.

The John Street Society

Upon persuasion by Barbara Heck, Phillip Embury assembled five persons in his home as his first congregation. Among his first worshippers was Beatty, a Negro servant of the Heck family. She became a charter member of the John Street Society. By the end of 1766, John Street Church had been established. In speaking of this church later, Hyde records:

> Two hundred and fifty names of subscribers are still preserved, among which are African maids—Dinahs and Chloes are in honor with the Livingstones and Delanceys, the blue blood of the time. Special mention must be made of Rachel, who gave nine shillings and Margaret contributed seven shillings.[19]

They were the caretakers of the parsonage.

Although statistics were not available by color prior to 1786, there were black members in Methodist Societies. In 1786, the general minutes recorded statistics by color. On July 20, 1787, John Street Church had 228 white members and 36 colored members in seventeen classes. The Saint

11

George Church reported 270 white members and 17 colored members. The largest Negro membership was on the Calvert Circuit. It had 505 white and 342 colored members. By 1786, there were 1,890 black members in the Methodist Episcopal Church. One thousand were in Antigua, West Indies.[20]

The Early Views of Methodism on Slavery

According to Bishop Matthew Simpson, "the relation of Methodism to the slave trade was from its beginning of antagonism." In his *Thoughts Upon Slavery* in 1774, Wesley wrote:

> I strike at the root of this complicated villainy. I absolutely deny all slave holding to be consistent with any degree of Natural justice . . . much less is it possible that any child of man should ever be born a slave. Liberty is the right of any human creature as soon as he breathes the vital air and no human can deprive him of the right.[21]

Wesley argued his case against slavery in terms of natural justice. He concurred with Locke and Jefferson that liberty was the right of every human creature as soon as he was born. He wrote his prohibition to slavery in the General Rules.

The one outstanding exception among the early Methodist leaders was George Whitefield. On March 22, 1751, he wrote a letter to John Wesley from Bristol, England justifying slavery:

> As for the lawfulness of keeping slaves, I have no doubt, since I hear of some that were brought with Abraham's money and some that were born in his house. I also cannot keep thinking that some of these servants mentioned by the Apostle in the epistles were, or had been slaves. It is plain that the Gibeonites were doomed to perpetual slavery; and though liberty is a sweet thing to such as are born free, yet to those who never knew the sweets of it, slavery, perhaps may not be irksome; however this be, it is plain to a demonstration that some countries cannot

12

be cultivated without Negroes. What a flourishing country might Georgia be had the use of them been permitted years ago. How many white people have been destroyed for want of them?[22]

How can George Whitefield, the flaming evangelist, utter such expression? He looked upon slavery as a double blessing. It was a blessing for the white man for he needed laborers in so hot a climate. He looked upon slavery as a blessing for the Negro because it gave the Negro a chance to be Christianized. Whitefield advocated the emancipation of the Negro's soul while it remained in an imprisoned body. A Negro was only an economic commodity. George Whitefield was long on evangelism but short on social action.

It is believed that George Whitefield exerted a powerful influence in introducing slavery in Georgia in 1749. When the colony was established by George II in 1732, slavery was excluded from its borders. According to Bishop Simpson, Whitefield owned seventy-five slaves when he died. In his will, he provided that his estate with all its buildings, lands, and Negroes would go to that elect body, that Mother of Israel, the Right Honorable Selina Countess Dowager of Huntingdon.

George Whitefield, the slaveholder, was one of the great preachers during the Great Awakening. According to record, he did not start a single church. He was not an organizer but a "suitcase evangelist."

In speaking of George Whitefield, Gregory records the following statement:

> The Prince of Perfervid Preachers, he had wrought great things through his might rushing eloquence but infinitely greater through the power from on high that was given to him. In Great Britain, multitudes of souls had been given to him. His genius was essentially different from Wesley's. If the latter could not vie with Whitefield's impassioned rhetoric, the former possessed no capacity for organization.[23]

The First Official Action On Slavery

The Baltimore Conference was the first conference to raise the question about slavery. In 1780, the conference included question seventeen: "Does this conference acknowledge that slavery is contrary to the law of God, man and nature and hurtful to society?" The answer was yes.

Contrary to later views, slavery was in the beginning of Methodism a moral matter. Slavery had an ill effect upon persons enslaved as well as upon the slaveholder.

This conference recognized further that it had a bounden duty to do something about slavery. It believed that it should start with the traveling preachers. Question sixteen was asked of the forty-two slave-holding preachers: "Ought not this conference require those traveling preachers who hold slaves to give promise to set them free?" The answer was yes. This answer was unequivocal. It was not contingent upon the civil law of the areas which they resided.

In addition, the continuing concern for the spiritual welfare of the slaves was also expressed. Question twenty-five was asked: "Ought not the assistant to meet with the colored people himself and appoint as helpers in his absence proper white persons and not suffer them to stay late and meet by themselves?" The answer again was yes.

The reason for this, according to T. B. Neeley, was to give the preachers an opportunity to preach to the slaves without arousing the suspicion of the owners. The slave owners were fearful that the slaves would devise schemes to gain their freedom.

In 1783, the Methodist Society took action regarding slave-holding by local preachers. Question twelve was asked: "What shall be done with our local preachers who hold slaves contrary to the laws which authorize their freedom in any of the United States?"

The answer was: "We will try them another year. In the meantime, let every assistant deal faithfully and plainly with

14

everyone and report to the next conference. It may then be necessary to suspend them."

The Wesleyan anti-slavery doctrine was very strong in the Methodist societies. Prior to the organization of the Methodist Episcopal Church, with the exception of George Whitefield, there was not a strong advocate of slavery among the early itinerant preachers. Freeborn Garretson believed that the day following his conversion he was commanded by God to set his slaves free. Hatch inherited slaves, but he too emancipated his slaves. William McKendree, during his early ministry, violently opposed both the slave trade and slaveholding. Jesse Lee also had strong convictions against slavery. Francis Asbury and Thomas Coke opposed slavery in the beginning. However, some of these men compromised their views later as slavery became more entrenched and more profitable. This will be covered in a later chapter.

Methodism was very appealing indeed to the men of color because of its evangelistic appeal and its stand upon the slave question. It was the belief of H. Richard Niebuhr that the position that Methodism took against slavery and its efforts to exclude slave-holders from its membership attracted Negroes to the church. According to Carter G. Woodson, it was the evangelistic note which appealed to the untutored mind.

CHAPTER II

The Negro in the Methodist Episcopal Church Before the Schism, 1784–1844

Prior to 1784, Methodism was composed of societies. There was no formal organization. As the societies grew, a need emerged to organize into some structure.

The Christmas Conference

The Methodist Episcopal Church was organized in 1784. On December 24, 1784, in the city of Baltimore, Maryland, this Christmas conference was called into session at 10:00 A.M. The conference convened in Lovely Lane Chapel. It was not a delegated body. There were about sixty ministers present at this historic session.[1] Among those present were Black Harry and Richard Allen to add technicolor to the memorable occasion.

The first order of business was the reading of Wesley's circular letter of instruction. The conference adopted this as the working agenda. On motion of John Dickens, the conference resolved the American societies into the Methodist Episcopal church.[2] Secondly, Asbury recommended that they would have superintendents, elders, and deacons.[3]

The next item of business dealt with ministerial relations. Francis Asbury was elected and ordained a deacon on December 24 by Coke, Whatcoat, and Vasey. He was elected and ordained an elder on December 25. He was elected superintendent unanimously on December 26 and was consecrated by Coke and Phillip Otterbein, a minister of a German congregation. Ten other men were ordained elders in order that they could travel and administer the sacraments to the people.

The third item on the agenda was the approval of a Book of Discipline. The conference accepted the revised form of the Episcopal prayer book prepared by Mr. Wesley. It approved the twenty-four Articles of Religion recommended by him. The conference added an additional article which declared the allegiance of the new church to the new republic.

The conference went on record as declaring its allegiance to John Wesley during his life and obeying him in matters of church government.[4] It pledged to continue a fraternal relation with the Methodists of the Old World.

The Methodist Episcopal Church was prophetic on social issues in its first session. Question forty-two was raised: What methods can we take to extirpate slavery? The answer:

> We are deeply conscious of the impropriety of making new terms of communion for a religious society already established, excepting on the most pressing occasion: and such we esteem the practice of holding our fellow creatures in slavery. We view it as contrary to the Golden Law of God on which hang all the Laws and the Prophets and the inalienable rights of mankind, as well as every principle of the revolution to hold in the deepest debasement in a more abject slavery than is perhaps to be found in any part of the world except America, so many souls that are capable of the Image of God.
> We therefore think that our bounden duty to take immediately some effectual method to extirpate this abomination from among us.[5]

This resolution was passed by the Christmas Conference, but it was not a unanimous decision. Jesse Lee says that many church members, local preachers, and even some of the itinerant preachers were opposed to the resolution.

17

The conference approved also a strategy to achieve the intent of the resolution:

(1) Every member of our society who are slave owners must free them within twelve months after they have been duly notified by the assistants of this action.
(2) Each assistant must keep a record of the names and ages of all slaves belonging to masters in their circuits.
(3) Members who refuse to follow the rules shall have the liberty to withdraw from the society.
(4) No person who voluntarily withdraws or who has been expelled from the society shall be eligible to receive the Lord's Supper.
(5) No person owning slaves shall in the future be admitted in the society or share in the Lord's Supper until the conditions stated above shall be met.

The Methodist societies had taken action previously regarding itinerant ministers and local preachers. This was the first action regarding church members. It was significant that this action was taken in the first General Conference.

These rules approved by the Christmas Conference met with some favorable reaction. Favorable approval was emerging in society. Two powerful antislavery influences were now developing. Growing out of the eighteenth century revival was an increased humanitarian impulse. This influence was strongest in England but had an impact upon American society as well. Another antislavery influence was the so-called revolutionary philosophy, "All men are by nature free and independent and that all men have the right to life, liberty, and the pursuit of happiness."[6] The effect of these two influences produced the first antislavery movement in America. Leaders of the New Republic had advocated the abolition of slavery. Jefferson denounced slavery as a system endangering the principle of liberty. Patrick Henry declared, "I will not— I cannot justify it." In 1786, Washington expressed a hope that a plan might be devised to abolish slavery.

New Attitudes Toward Slavery

The invention of the cotton gin by Eli Whitney in 1793, produced an attitudinal change in the North and the South. The cotton gin became an economic asset for the whites in the South, but it tightened the rope of slavery around the Negroes' neck. The cotton boom stimulated the rapid rise of cotton mills in New England. By 1810, there were eighty-seven domestic mills in New England. Hence, cotton was producing a new economic base for both the South and the North. In addition, Britain became a market for the raw material.

Slavery became more entrenched. In 1780, it seemed evident that slavery would be abolished due to the impulse of freedom inherent in the American Revolution. By 1800, all states had forbidden the importation of slaves but, the economic factor had now made slavery indeed more profitable. "In 1790, good Negroes could be purchased for $300." By 1830, the price of slaves was $1,200. By 1860, the price of slaves had sky-rocketed to $2,000.[7]

The great slave traders were from New England. Providence and Newport in Rhode Island were great slave markets. Slaves were sold to the South for the following reasons: (1) The climate of New England was inhospitable to Africans; (2) the plantation system was unsuitable to the North; (3) white workers opposed unfair competition from the slaves; (4) strong religious opposition by the Quakers on moral grounds.[8] By 1750, nine-tenths of slaves were found in the southern states. By 1804, all northern states had abolished slavery.

The southern states began to develop a rationalization for slavery. States had enacted laws permitting slavery and forbidding the emancipation of slaves. Some argued that slavery was a part of the Divine Economy for Negroes (Genesis 9:22, 25-27 and Ephesians 6:5, Colossians 3:22). Other advanced the argument that slaves were better off than some white laborers.

While slavery was becoming more institutionalized in the South, a new and more aggressive antislavery movement was arising in the North. These movements sprang up in churches and secular organizations as well.

Foremost in the antislave movement was the fearless leader, William Lloyd Garrison. He began his paper called the *Liberator* in 1831. On one occasion, Garrison wrote words of encouragement to the oppressed. He said:

> Your condition, as a people has long attracted my attention, secured my efforts, and awakened in my breast a flame of sympathy which neither the winds nor the waves of opposition can ever extinguish. . . . It is the fewness of your friends—the multitude of your enemies—that induces me to stand forth in your defense.[9]

Garrison had a pervasive influence upon New England Methodism. Orange Scott of Vermont, a leading Methodist minister, supported the abolition movement. *Zion's Herald* became a leading newspaper that used the printer's ink to fight slavery. The fight continued unabated.

General Conference Actions on the Slave Question, 1808–1840

By 1808, anything pertaining to slave-holding among members had been eliminated from the Book of Discipline. Instead, slavery ceased to be a connectional interest affecting the whole Methodist Episcopal Church. The General Conference passed a resolution authorizing each annual conference to "form its own regulations relative to buying or selling slaves." Another unusual motion prevailed ordering 1,000 Disciplines to be printed for use in South Carolina in which the section dealing with slavery would be omitted.

The 1816 General Conference can best be described as

the "Conference of Great Compromise." The General Conference adopted the following:

> Your committee finds that in the South and West the civil authorities render emancipation impracticable and . . . they are constrained to admit that to bring about such change in the civil code as would favor the cause of liberty is not in the power of the General Conference . . . they beg to submit the following resolution:
> Resolved . . . No slave holder shall be eligible to any official station in our church hereafter where the laws of the state in which he lives will admit of emancipation and permit the liberated slave to enjoy freedom.[10]

The 1824 General Conference added three new paragraphs that related to the ministry of Negroes:

(1) All our preachers shall prudently enforce upon our members the necessity of teaching their slaves to read the word of God; and to allow them time to attend upon the public worship of God on regular days of divine service.

(2) Our colored preachers and official members shall have the privileges which are usual to others in the district and quarterly conferences where the usages of the country do not forbid it and presiding elders may hold for them separate district conferences where the colored local preachers will justify it.

(3) The Annual Conference may employ colored preachers to travel and preach where their services are judged necessary: provided that no one shall be so employed without having been recommended according to the form of the Discipline.[11]

A phrase which became common in Disciplinary language was, "We declare that we are ever convinced of the great evil of slavery." It was put in the Discipline in 1824 and remained in the Discpline until 1860.

In 1828, a resolution was presented to the General Conference providing that any slaveholder who treated his slaves inhumanely either by refusing them proper care, or

21

separation by means of purchase and sale of members of families, should be brought to trial as in case of immorality. The motion was placed on the table and never removed.

The 1836 General Conference met in Cincinnati, Ohio. It was indeed a heated session. Many laymen and ministers from all sections of the country were convinced that The Church could no longer wink upon slavery. Slavery had to be faced as a moral issue. Many memorials were presented to the General Conference. These were referred to a special committee. The special committee made the following report to the General Conference: "That it is not expedient to make any change in our Book of Discipline respecting slavery, and that we deem it improper further to agitate the subject in the General Conference at present."[12]

Two fraternal delegates attended this General Conference. William Lord of the British Conference and William Case of the Wesleyan Methodist church in upper Canada criticized slavery sharply. William Lord's criticism was that slavery in a "Christian State" is in violation of great scripture principles and the precepts of Christianity. He expressed an ardent hope that the Methodist Episcopal Church would be able to lead public opinion, a unanimous rejection of slavery and its social mischiefs on the ground of its repugnancy to the Law of Christ. This address was so stinging that it was not published in the official minutes of the conference of 1836.

A committee was raised by the General Conference to prepare a rebuttal to this stinging criticism and a pastoral letter to the people. The committee was composed of Nathan Bang, William Capers and Thomas A. Morris. The following is an excerpt from this report:

> These facts . . . constrain us as your pastors . . . to exhort you to abstain from all abolition movements and associations and to refrain from patronizing any of their publications.
>
> We have come to the solemn conviction that the only safe scriptural and prudent way for us both as ministers and

people . . . is wholly to refrain from this agitating subject which is now convulsing the country, and consequently The Church from end to end.[13]

This report was approved by the General Conference by an overwhelming vote of 122 to 11.

During the 1836-40 quadrennium, the slave struggle was intensified. In almost all annual conferences, it came up in one way or another. The abolitionists were determined to win, but the bishops ruled harshly. In some cases, the bishops refused to place petitions dealing with slavery on the calendar of the annual conferences. They believed that abolition of slavery was being promoted by dangerous radicals.

Most of the abolitionists were "young Turks." Some were refused admission to annual conferences because they favored abolition. Others were suspended from the annual conference for attending antislave meetings.

The 1840 General Conference closed with no significant action on the slave question. The Southerners felt that they had now buried the issue forever. Some of the abolitionists felt also that it was a futile effort. A few withdrew from the church and formed the Wesleyan Methodist church.[14]

The 1844 General Conference

The memorable 1844 General Conference was convened in Green Street Church, New York on May 1. Thirty-three annual conferences had 180 delegates. Only a few radicals were among the delegates from either the North or South.

This conference was besieged with memorials and resolutions on slavery—pro and con. The Episcopal Address made no mention of this burning issue. Instead the Episcopal Address emphasized missionary work among Negroes.[15]

A delaying tactic was used. Three days passed before a committee was appointed to consider these memorials.

The first issue debated in the General Conference was

the appeal of F. A. Harding. It was the order of the day for May 7. Mr. Harding was appealing against the decision of the Baltimore Conference. He was suspended from the Baltimore Conference for refusing to manumit certain slaves that he had inherited through marriage. This case was debated for five days. Finally, the vote was called. The Baltimore Conference was sustained by a vote of 117 to 56.[16] This test case showed that the conference was predominantly composed of members who were opposed to slavery. This led the way for the Andrew case.

On May 20, 1844, the Andrew case came before the General Conference from the Committee on Episcopacy. Bishop Andrew was a slave owner. A lady from Augusta, Georgia, had bequeathed a girl to the bishop on condition that he should liberate her and send her to Liberia at the age of maturity. The girl refused to go to Liberia and therefore remained property of the bishop. He had also inherited slaves from his first and second marriage which the Georgia law prohibited him from setting free.

Sincere efforts were made by some to reach a responsible compromise. Four of the bishops—Soule, Hedding, Waugh, and Morris—signed a statement for consideration by the General Conference as a compromise. Before it was debated on the conference floor, the abolitionists persuaded Bishop Hedding to remove his name. Since the report was not signed by all bishops, the conference voted to table it by 95 to 84.

Some of the lawmakers felt that unity was more important than the emancipation of the slaves. Others were convinced that owning slaves was contrary to the Law of God. God's Law should therefore take precedence over the laws of the states. The issue could not be resolved. Compromise is never possible when right meets wrong at a right angle.

After days of animated debate, the main motion was called "Resolved that he, (Bishop Andrew), would desist from the exercise of his office as long as this impediment remain." The determinative resolution was passed with 111 yeas and 69 nays. One voted in the affirmative from the

24

slave-holding section of the church. Seventeen of the negative votes came from the non-slave-holding conference. On June 1, 1844, Bishop Andrew was suspended from the episcopacy of the Methodist Episcopal church.[17]

After sixty years, the Methodist Episcopal church divided into two denominations. The Methodist Episcopal Church South was located chiefly below the Mason-Dixon Line. The Church North served the area above the Mason-Dixon Line.

CHAPTER III

The Lull After the Storm, 1845–1863

The 1844 General Conference may be described as the conference in which "The Great Schism" occurred in Methodism. By its vote on The Plan of Separation, it authorized two new denominations.

The period of 1845–1863 may be called the "lull after the storm." It was also a period of readjustment and reorganization.

When the Northern delegates returned home, they were confronted with a rising tide of disapproval of the action of the General Conference. Some churchmen questioned the constitutionality of the action. They held that the plan could only be consummated by vote of the several annual conferences; but Nathan Bang, an architect of the plan, argued that the General Conference was the sole judge of the validity of its action. The General Conference was both the legislative body and the judicial body of the Church.

The Southern churchmen returned home bewildered and smarting under a feeling of defeat. They had gone to the conference fully confident that the slave question had been settled forever in the 1840 General Conference. That was only a lull before the storm.

The National Effect of the Schism in the Church

The division in the Methodist Episcopal church planted a seed that perhaps eventuated in the division of the nation. Many political leaders deplored this schism in the church. They feared it would lead to a rift in the nation.

In these words, Henry Clay expressed his perturbation:

> I would not say that such a separation would necessarily produce a dissolution of the political union but the example would be fraught with imminent danger.[1]

William H. Seward regarded the schism in the Church as a "sinister prophecy."

A New Start

Both churches had to start anew. The Northern conferences united in a concerted effort to make Methodism a strong bulwark against slavery. Antislave movements developed rapidly within the Church. In addition abolition societies grew up outside the church like mushrooms. All conferences passed resolutions taking affirmative action about slavery. In addition, the Church North began to increase its ministry to the Negroes in their territory.

The Church South confined its missionary work primarily to the slave population. It redoubled its zeal and efforts on behalf of the slaves. By 1849, fifteen annual conferences of the Church South had established African Missions. There were 122 missionaries at work among the slave population. A conservative estimate is that the Church South spent $1,320,778 from 1845 to 1860 on these plantation missions.[2]

The outstanding leaders in these missionary efforts were William Capers of South Carolina, Atticus G. Haygood of

Georgia, and William Winans of Mississippi. On one occasion, Dr. Winans defended the religion of the South in these words:

> The religion of the South . . . does . . . just what the Savior and His apostles did when they preached the whole of . . . true religion in countries where slavery prevailed.[3]

Location of Black People in Methodism

Most of the Negroes lived below the Mason-Dixon Line. In 1843, there were 145,409 black members of the Methodist Episcopal Church.[4] This number constituted about 12% of the total church membership. Only 13,464 blacks lived in the boundaries of the fifteen northern conferences. Below Mason-Dixon Line lived 95,282 black Methodists. More than two-thirds were found in Alabama, Georgia, and South Carolina. There were 39,495 black Methodists in South Carolina alone.

The border states, Kentucky, Missouri, Virginia, Maryland, and Delaware, had a combined black Methodist membership of 36,663. Twenty-five percent of black Methodism resided in these border states.

The border states were slave-holding states, but they were also related economically to the North.

For most of these states, the people were divided over the slave issue. However, Virginia was the only state which seceded from the Union. Even in that state the people were not unanimous.

This region may be described as the "buffer zone" area. Both denominations looked upon it as the "uncommitted area." It was therefore handled with "kid gloves."

This area produced some real problems for administrators. Many churches in Virginia, Kentucky, and Missouri were opposed to being related to Southern Methodism. Contrariwise, there were churches equally opposed to being connected with the Methodist Episcopal Church. In the state of Missouri, both denominations had three annual conferences.[5]

In 1845, Bishop Thomas A. Morris was urged to organize a fourth annual conference for the Methodist Episcopal Church. He refused the invitation for two reasons: First, hatred was so rife; in speaking of this matter, the bishop said: "You can reason with a man's judgment but not with his passion." Second, the Articles of Separation forbade it in these words:

All societies, stations and conferences adhering to the Church in the South by a vote of the majority of the members . . . shall remain under the unmolested pastoral care of the Southern Church, and the ministers of the Methodist Episcopal Church shall in no wise attempt to organize churches or societies within the limits of the Church South nor shall they attempt to exercise pastoral oversight therein.[6]

The 1848 General Conference

Among other actions of the General Conference of 1848, was the revocation of the Plan of Separation. This action was based upon a petition received from the border states. This petition recommended the annulment based upon the following reasons: (1) there was no justifiable reason for the Plan of Separation; (2) the Methodist Church South had already violated the agreement in establishing churches in the domain of the Methodist Episcopal church; and (3) annual conferences did not ratify the plan.

The revocation of the Plan of Separation by this General Conference made possible the return of the Methodist Episcopal Church to the southern region of the nation. There were bishops and other churchmen who did not concur in this action. Hence, there was only limited missionary work by the Methodist Episcopal Church in this region. This denomination did work more feverishly in the border states.

The 1856 General Conference

The General Conference of the Methodist Episcopal Church convened in Indianapolis, Indiana, in 1856. Several petitions were placed on the calendar to change the General Rules on Slavery.

One memorable speech made in favor of changing the General Rules was by Edward Thomson of the Ohio Conference. The following words are excerpts from this speech:

> Is it right that one man should hold another as property? . . . What is man? A moral, rational, immortal accountable being—capable of moral discernment—acting under a moral law with a moral nature. . . . The New Testament is not pro-slavery, it is not even tolerant of it. The mistake made by Asbury, when he lowered the standard of the Discipline to establish the Church in the South, was one of the greatest mistakes ever made by any mortal man. . . . If Asbury could see the results of his course, he would weep. . . . Will the Church in the South ever rise up and take her stand in favor of emancipation, while there are ministers, bishops . . . who are justifying slavery?[7]

This conference did not succeed in changing the General Rules. Perhaps it failed to change the Discipline because of its desire to woo the border conferences. It did however leave in the Discipline this cliche: "We declare that we are as much as ever convinced of the great evil of slavery."

The black Methodists came back to this conference to press their claim for independent churches and black preachers. A Negro member of the Sharp Street Church, Baltimore, Maryland, John A. Collins, presented the Memorial to the General Conference.[8] The request was first made in 1848. Again the General Conference voted nonconcurrence. It did approve of black people having separate quarterly conferences when it was in the judgment of the presiding elder to be expedient.

The General Conference of 1860

The Buffalo General Conference could not delay any longer revising the General Rules. No longer was it able to pacify the border conferences.

This conference was flooded with petitions. There were 811 petitions signed by 45,857 persons requesting that the Discipline would be amended. Likewise, there were 137 petitions with 3,999 signatures requesting that the General Rules would remain unchanged. A cursory examination of these petitions shows that more people now approved of amending the Discipline.

The Dred Scott Decision had also an impact upon this General Conference. Prior to the decision of the Supreme Court and in anticipation of it, President James Buchanan, in his inaugural address on March 4, 1857, appealed to the citizens to accept the verdict of the Court whatever it may be.

On March 6, 1857, Chief Justice Roger B. Taney announced the decision of the Court. By a seven to two vote, Dred Scott was denied his freedom on the ground that he was a slave in Missouri and a slave was not entitled to sue. By its ruling, Negroes were considered as inanimate objects—without rights to be respected and guaranteed by the Declaration of Independence.

Strong reactions to the decision were instantaneous. Defiance of the Court's order was proclaimed by the newspaper. The appeal of President Buchanan fell on deaf ears in the North. Some Northern Methodist vowed that the church must prove that Negroes do have rights as others.

After many hours of animated debate, the General Conference amended the Discipline by adding the following paragraph:

> We believe that the buying, selling or holding of human beings as chattels is contrary to the Law of God and Nature; inconsistent with the Golden Rule. . . . We therefore affectionately admonish all our preachers and people to keep

themselves pure from this great evil and to seek its extirpation by all lawful and Christian means.[9]

The adoption of this amendment was protested strongly by the border conferences. Many left the General Conference before adjournment. As a result of their leaving, it became necessary for the conference to adjourn on June 4 due to lack of a quorum. This is at least the second time in the Methodist Church that a General Conference had to adjourn due to the lack of a quorum. On May 24, 1816, the General Conference adjourned early also for the same reason.

Because of the action of the General Conferences, several members and preachers withdrew from the Methodist Episcopal Church. Some joined the Methodist Episcopal Church South.

At the close of this General Conference, the following may be said about the Methodist Episcopal Church:

(1) When these people withdrew from the church, the Methodist Episcopal Church was now almost unanimous in its opposition to slavery;
(2) Majority of the members were in free states.
(3) Most members of the church now would support any movement to eliminate slavery from the nation.

CHAPTER IV

The Period of Institutional Development, 1864–1900

The last three decades of the nineteenth century may be described as the Period of Institutional Development. The nation had just undergone a bloody war between the states. Many lives were lost and much property destroyed. It was the period of beginning anew.

The Methodist Episcopal Church had been affected by the war. It had lost members in the war. In 1864, it had a total membership of 984,933 members in 26 states and the District of Columbia.[1] There were 28,634 black members in the Church. The Methodist Episcopal Church had 56 conferences. Only 8 conferences reported black members. There were only a few black members in the Deep South. Most members lived in the northern and border states.

The 1864 General Conference

The General Conference of the Methodist Church convened in Philadelphia, Pennsylvania on May 2, 1864. High on its agenda was the planning for the evangelization of the blacks in the South. As victory seemed imminent for the Union Army, this conference began to perfect its plan to invade the South with teachers and missionaries.

The quesions foremost in the minds of the delegates were: (1) What shall we do for the Negroes? (2) How can we best minister to them?

Three views were enunciated: (1) Negroes should be encouraged to unite with the independent Negro branches of Methodism; (2) ecclesiastical equality was advocated—this was indeed a minority viewpoint; and (3) establishment of mission conferences for Negroes in the church.[2] One writer vindicated this view in these words:

> Such separate conferences were essential, too, because it was believed that through them the greatest good could be accomplished. We have for the same reason our German conferences and our Scandinavian, French and Welsh Missions.[3]

After several days of debate, the conference approved the resolution to establish mission conferences for Negroes in the church.[4] It also approved of the necessary enabling legislation in order that these mission conferences could be organized.[5]

First Black Man Admitted Into a White Annual Conference

The New England Conference is credited with being the first conference to establish an open door policy for conference membership. It admitted John N. Mars into the conference on March 30, 1864. Bishop Edward R. Ames was the presiding officer. It is significant to note that this action was taken prior to the convening of the 1864 General Conference.

This first black candidate for the itinerant ministry was born on June 22, 1804, in Norfolk, Connecticut. His parents were slaves and were owned by a Presbyterian minister. They obtained their freedom at a price of $1,800.

At the age of twenty, John was converted. Shortly

34

afterwards, he was licensed to preach. Later the New York Conference ordained him a local deacon.

In 1840, he went to Salem, Massachusetts, to assist the Reverend W. S. Spaulding in a revival. Many persons were converted in this revival. He settled in Salem and served as pastor of the colored church. Still later, he served as a missionary in Canada to the colored people who had escaped.

After he was received on trial, his first appointment was Clinton, Massachusetts. In October, 1864, he was transferred to the newly created Washington Annual Conference. He was appointed to Sharp Street Church. In 1866, he was appointed presiding elder of the Chesapeake district in the Washington Conference. He served in this capacity for four years. In 1870, he transferred back to the New England Conference. He was appointed as conference missionary. He retired in 1873. On September 17, 1884, he died at Athol, Massachusetts.[6]

The Organization of Black Conferences, 1864–1868

The responsibility was assigned by the Board of Bishops to several bishops to organize these black conferences. In many conferences, the men of color were unable to read or write. Some white ministers from several white conferences were lent to these conferences on a lend lease basis for a period of time.

THE DELAWARE MISSION CONFERENCE

The first Negro mission conference to be organized was the Delaware Conference. Its first session was convened in John Wesley Church (Tindley Temple) in Philadelphia, Pennsylvania on July 29, 1864.[7] Bishop Edmund S. Janes organized the conference. Its first secretary was W. S. Elzey.

It was constituted of the colored churches and colored

35

preachers who preferred to be in their own conference and associated together in conference relations. For many years, they had sent memorials to the General Conference to authorize this preference.

In speaking of this request, Bishop Matthew Simpson gave two reasons for it: (1) colored people preferred to meet in distinct congregations and separate conferences for they felt that they were not treated as equal in mixed congregations or conferences; and (2) the desire for more intimate association with each other in all church arrangement. In addition, this fellowship would provide for the Negroes the only technique to develop within themselves a sense of worth.

Its boundary was determined by the presiding bishop. It was established to include the territory east and north of the Washington conference, the principal part being the state of Delaware and eastern Maryland with a few churches in New Jersey and Pennsylvania.

The following men were charter members of the conference: Joshua Brinkley, Isaiah Broughton, Samuel Dale, James Davis, Wilmore S. Elzey, Isaac Hinson, John G. Montuff, Frost Pallet, Jehu Pierce, Harrison Smith, and Nathan Young. Ten men were admitted on trial.

The conference organized with 21 preachers; 39 local preachers; 4,964 church members; 841 Sunday school scholars; and 34 churches.

WASHINGTON MISSION CONFERENCE

The second Negro mission conference to be organized was the Washington Conference. It was organized in Sharp Street Church, Baltimore, Maryland, on October 27, 1864 by Bishop Levi Scott.[8] Its first secretary was B. Brown.

Its boundary was set to include all the Negro work in western Maryland, the District of Columbia, the state of West Virginia, as much of Pennsylvania as lay west of the Susquehanna River, including the towns on the said river and portions of Virginia.

It was organized with 21 traveling elders; 43 local preachers; 8,194 church members; and 19 churches.

MISSISSIPPI MISSION CONFERENCE

The third black mission conference to be organized was the Mississippi Mission Conference. Prior to the organization of this conference, Bishop Edward R. Ames appointed John Paul Newman as the supervisor of the Missionary work in the southwest.[9] Prior to his appointment, he served the Washington Square Church, New York City. This supervisory responsibility included three states: Louisiana, Mississippi, and Texas.

On December 25, 1865, Bishop Edward Thomas convened the second Christmas Conference in Wesley Chapel, New Orleans, Louisiana on South Liberty Street at 9:00 A.M.[10]

Unlike the Delaware and Washington Conference, the original members of the Mississippi Mission Conference were all white ministers. They were on lend-lease from northern conferences. From the Northwest Indiana Conference was transferred Nelson L. Brakeman as missionary to Baton Rouge, Louisiana, and H. G. Jackson, as missionary to New Orleans. Joseph Welch was transferred from the Philadelphia Conference and W. M. Henry was received as a transfer from the Genessee Conference. The Reverend J. P. Newman transferred from the New York Conference. These were the charter members of the Mississippi Mission Conference.

On December 26, 1865, the following colored preachers were admitted on trial: James Bryant, David (Elias) Dibble, Henry Green, Thomas Kennedy, Scott Chinn, Samuel Osborne, Anthony Ross, Hardy Ryan, Samuel M. Small, Emperor Williams, and William Murrell. In addition, one white minister, Richard K. Diossey, was admitted on trial. His orders were recognized from the Methodist Protestant Church.

The conference was divided into four districts: New Orleans, Opelousas, Mississippi, and Texas. The ministers were assigned to places rather than to organized congregations. There were only three organized black congregations: Wesley, First Street, and Marais Street and two white congregations—Ames and Fourth Street.

There were 2,128 black church members and 88 white members. This conference gave birth to five other conferences—Louisiana, Mississippi, Texas, West Texas, and Upper Mississippi.

SOUTH CAROLINA MISSION CONFERENCE

The South Carolina Conference was organized on April 2, 1866 by Bishop Osmon C. Baker. It was organized in Charleston, South Carolina. The first secretary of the conference was Alonza Webster. He was a white minister on lend-lease from the Vermont Conference.[11]

The original members of the South Carolina Mission Conference were: T. Williard Lewis, Alonzo Webster, J. A. Sasportas, H. D. Owens, F. Smith, T. Phillips, W. J. Cole, W. J. Tripps, Mansfield French, A. D. Leavett, J. C. Emerson, Jack Grimke, J. C. Nixson, and L. Anders.

The bishop established the boundary of the conference to include the state of South Carolina, Eastern Georgia, and Florida. Two districts were constituted: Charleston, which included all of South Carolina, and Florida District which included all Florida and the eastern part of Georgia.

This conference was organized with 2,791 church members; 16 local preachers; 12 established congregations; and 14 ministers.

TENNESSEE MISSION CONFERENCE

The Tennessee Conference was organized at Murfreesboro, Tennessee, on October 11, 1866. Bishop D. W. Clark was the organizer. Its first secretary was W. H. Pearne.

Its boundary was established to include that portion of Tennessee not already included in the Holston Conference.

This conference was organized with 40 traveling preachers; 49 local preachers; and 3,173 church members. There were four districts. It was organized with 13 churches with an estimated value of $59,100.[12]

By the authority given by the 1876 General Conference, this conference was divided (not by changing boundaries) but allowing the separation of the white and colored work by a concurrent vote of both groups.

TEXAS MISSION CONFERENCE

On January 3, 1867, the Texas Mission Conference was organized in Houston, Texas. Bishop Matthew W. Simpson organized the conference. Its first secretary was Joseph Welch. It was the first offspring from the Mississippi Mission Conference.

The following men were transferred from the Mississippi Mission Conference: G. E. Brooks, J. Davis, David (Elias) Dibble and Joseph Welch. On credentials, George W. Honey was received from the Wesleyan Church. It was organized with three white ministers, twelve colored preachers and two German preachers.[13]

Three districts were established. It was organized with 1,093 full church members and 21 local preachers. Five congregations were already established.

GEORGIA MISSION CONFERENCE

On October 10, 1867, the Georgia Mission Conference was organized by Bishop D. W. Clark, in Atlanta, Georgia. Nine preachers were recognized as charter members. Two men were recognized as probationers. Twenty-three were admitted on trial at this session. Seven were received on credentials from the Methodist Episcopal Church South.

North Carolina Mission Conference

The North Carolina Conference was organized at Union Chapel in Alexandria City, North Carolina on January 14, 1868. Bishop Edward R. Ames was the organizer. Its first secretary was W. G. Tattow. It was organized with one district; 10 churches; 18 ministers; and 3,331 church members.

The 1868 General Conference

This conference was faced with a constitutional problem. There had been eight Negro mission conferences organized in the past quadrennium. These conferences elected delegates to participate in the 1868 General Conference.

In order for these delegates to be seated with a vote in the General Conference, it was necessary to modify the legislation adopted four years earlier. In 1864, the General Conference denied the following rights to mission conferences: (1) they could not send delegates to General Conference; (2) they could not draw dividends from the Book Concern; and they could not vote upon constitutional amendments.

The issue was debated for ten days. On May 11, 1868, the General Conference voted to rescind a portion of its 1864 legislation. The resolution was approved by 212 in favor and 14 opposed.[14] By this action, these Mission Conferences were given the status of Annual Conferences. It also allowed for the Provisional Delegates to be seated at that session of the General Conference.

There were only two Negro delegates elected from the eight mission conferences. They were James Davis, Delaware Conference, and Benjamin Brown from the Washington Conference.[15] They were the first blacks to be seated in the lawmaking body of the Methodist Episcopal Church.

Other Black Conferences Organized, 1868–1927

From 1868 to 1927, there were eleven conferences organized. All except one were organized in the Deep South. The South Florida Conference was the last to be organized.

THE MISSISSIPPI CONFERENCE

The Mississippi Conference was "the second offspring" of the Mississippi Mission Conference. It was organized on January 7, 1869, by Matthew W. Simpson in Asbury Church, Canton, Mississippi. Due to illness in his family, the bishop was detained for one day. In his absence, the Reverend James Lynch, a Negro presiding elder, was elected as temporary chairman. The Reverend A. C. McDonald, a white clergyman, president of Rust College, was elected as its first secretary.[16]

It was organized with two districts, Holy Springs and Jackson. The Reverend James Lynch and the Reverend A. C. McDonald served as a bi-racial team as presiding elders. Seven men were admitted in full connection, twenty men were admitted on trial. It began with a church membership of 8,732 members. Twenty-six congregations had already been established.

THE LOUISIANA CONFERENCE

The Louisiana Conference was the third offspring of the Mississippi Mission Conference. It was organized in Wesley Church, New Orleans, Louisiana, on January 13, 1869. Bishop M. W. Simpson was the organizer. Its first secretary was J. P. Newman, a white clergyman.

It organized with 37 ministers; 27 churches; and 10,662 church members in five districts.

THE LEXINGTON CONFERENCE

The Lexington Conference was organized at Harrodsburg, Kentucky on March 2, 1869 by Bishop Edward Thomson. E. C. Moore was elected as its first secretary. It was composed of colored ministers only. It was organized with 67 traveling preachers, 52 local preachers, 7,926 church members and 53 churches at an estimated value of $128,400.00.

The 1872 General Conference extended its boundary to include Ohio and Indiana. In 1876, its boundary was extended farther to include the state of Illinois. In 1920, its boundary was extended still farther to include Michigan, Wisconsin, and Minnesota.[17]

THE FLORIDA CONFERENCE

The Florida Conference was organized at Jacksonville, Florida on January 19, 1873. Bishop Edward R. Ames was the presiding bishop. Its first secretary was I. B. Darnell.

The boundary was established to include all the state of Florida, except that portion lying west of the Appalachicola River.

It was organized with 29 preachers; 59 local preachers; 27 Sunday schools; and 1,033 scholars. There were already established 33 churches and 2,207 church members.

THE WEST TEXAS CONFERENCE

The West Texas Conference was organized in Wesley Church, Austin, Texas, on January 22, 1874 by Bishop Thomas Bowman. Its first secretary was G. W. Honey, a white clergyman.[18]

42

The following men were charter members of the conference: G. W. Honey, Jacob Miller, Mack Henson, Daniel Gregory, Samuel Allen, W. D. Sheeley, Larkin Capper, Archie Johnson, J. T. Hill, T. T. Leach, T. G. Lacy, Alex Campbell, London Morris, Isaac Wright, Cyprus Hatchett, Daniel Harper, and Charles Scruggs.

The West Texas Conference embraced the Negro work in that part of Texas which was not included in the Texas Conference, and also included any mission work in New Mexico.

It was organized with 5,338 church members, 21 churches, and 3 districts.

The Central Alabama Conference

The Central Alabama Conference was organized on October 18, 1876, at Corn House Camp Ground in Randolph County near Wedowee, Alabama. Bishop Levi Scott was the organizer; A. S. Lakin, a white minister, was the secretary.[19]

It included the Dadeville, Marion and Huntsville Districts, formerly belonging to the Alabama Conference. It created a new district called Springfield. It was then constituted as a black conference. It organized with 43 preachers; 41 churches; and 5,932 church members in four districts.

The Savannah Conference

From 1866 to 1876, the Negro work in Georgia was a part of the Georgia Conference. On November 1, 1876, the Savannah Conference was organized. It was organized in Augusta, Georgia by Bishop Levi Scott. The first secretary was C. E. Fisher.

When organized it had 118 ministers; 146 churches; and 9,728 church members in five districts.

LITTLE ROCK CONFERENCE

The Little Rock Conference was organized in Van Buren, Arkansas on February 21, 1879. The presiding bishop was Edward G. Andrew. Its first secretary was I. G. Pollard.[20]

Its boundary was established to include Negro work in Arkansas. The conference was organized with 2 districts; 22 ministers; 23 churches; and 1,362 members.

On December 3, 1929, the Little Rock Conference became the Southwest Conference. Bishop M. W. Clair, Sr., was the organizer of this conference. Its boundary was extended to include the colored work in Oklahoma.

EAST TENNESSEE CONFERENCE

The East Tennessee Conference was organized on October 25, 1880, by Bishop Erastus O. Haven.[21] It was organized in Greenville, Tennessee. Its first secretary was B. H. Johnson.

The following men were charter members: C. K. Mays, J. J. Harris, D. B. Lewton, William Buford, W. H. Roberts, A. J. Fletcher, O. W. Hypshire, Alexander Jordan, W. M. Mills, Alexander Gillespie, J. C. Tate, J. W. Walls, James Varnell, Alexander Lindsey, and C. Shaw.

Originally, its boundary was to include the territory in East Tennessee not included in the Tennessee Conference. Later, its boundary was extended to include seventeen counties of Virginia formerly in the Washington Conference and parts of West Virginia.

The conference organized with 17 ministers; 24 churches; and 2,491 church members in two districts.

THE CENTRAL MISSOURI CONFERENCE

The Central Missouri Conference was organized on March 24, 1887, in Sedalia, Missouri. It was organized by

Bishop W. F. Mallalieu.[22] Its first secretary was J. W. Jackson.

It was organized as a result of the Enabling Act of 1884 which granted permission to the colored members of the Saint Louis Conference and Missouri Conference to organize into a Negro conference.

Its first boundary included all colored work in Missouri. In 1928, a new boundary was established to include the states of Kansas, Colorado, and Nebraska. These states had formerly been a part of the Lincoln Conference. In 1928, the name of the conference was changed from Central Missouri to Central West Conference.

It was organized with 54 ministers; 83 churches; and 6,031 church members in three districts.

THE UPPER MISSISSIPPI CONFERENCE

The Upper Mississippi Conference was organized in Asbury Church, Holly Springs, Mississippi on February 5, 1891. Bishop Edward Gayer Andrews presided over the organization session. The first secretary of the conference was J. L. Wilson.[23]

The boundary was established to include the Negro work in Mississippi not included in the Mississippi Conference. It also included a few white ministers and congregations in Mississippi.

It was organized with 17,131 church members; 88 pastoral charges; 74 ministers in full connection; and 17 men on probation.

THE ATLANTA CONFERENCE

On January 22, 1896, the Savannah Conference was divided in Griffin, Georgia, into the Savannah and Atlanta Conferences.

On January 21, 1897, the Atlanta Conference was

45

organized in the Lloyd Street Church (Central) in Atlanta by Bishop Cyrus D. Foss. The first secretary was R. J. Adams.[24]

It was organized with 65 ministers; 141 churches; and 13,502 church members in four districts.

THE SOUTH FLORIDA CONFERENCE

The last of the Negro conferences to be organized was the South Florida Conference. It had been the South Florida Mission since 1873.

In 1924, the General Conference granted permission for the mission to be organized into a conference upon a vote of the majority of the members present and voting.

On January 22, 1925, Bishop E. G. Richardson organized the South Florida Conference at Bradenton, Florida. Its first secretary was W. P. Pickens.[25]

It included the colored work in that part of Florida lying south of parallel 29, including New Smyrna Beach, Daytona Beach, Ormond Beach, and Deland.

It organized with two districts: Atlantic and Gulf. There were 33 ministers; 34 churches; and 3,385 church members.

Board of Home Mission and Church Extension

From 1865 to 1884, the Board of Church Extension had assisted 1,117 Negro congregations in the erection of their first churches. It had by 1884, disbursed a grand total of $181,952.95 in donations and $111,539 in loans to these fifteen conferences.[26]

The black people were not only recipients of donations and loans, but they contributed to the fund themselves. In 1884, these black conferences contributed a grand total of $22,109.84 to the church extension fund. Although this was a small amount compared to what they received, it represented sacrifices when measured against the income of these poverty-stricken, recently emancipated people.

In addition to assisting these black congregations in the erection of their first churches, the missionary department gave missionary appropriations to black churches. It was recommended further that appropriations would be made to charges annually but not to exceed five years. For the quadrennium 1880–1883, the Missionary Department disbursed $241,950 in missionary appropriations to the black conferences.[27]

The Origin and Development of
Black Institutions of Learning

It was the opinion of Carter G. Woodson that Reconstruction began in the school houses and not in the state houses. The Methodist Episcopal Church shared this viewpoint. In its fifth report, the Freedmen's Aid Society declared:

True the chains which bound their hand and fettered their limbs were broken; but ignorance, vice and oppression had forged fetters for the soul that the act of Emancipation could not sunder. A dash of the pen made them free but it could not make them intelligent and moral.

THE FREEDMEN'S AID SOCIETY—
THE METHODIST WAY OF CURING ILLITERACY

The Freedmen's Aid Society was organized in 1866. On May 7, 1866, a group of ministers and laymen were called to Cincinnati, Ohio, to consider the relief and education of the freedmen.

This society was approved by the Annual Conference in 1867 and the General Conference of 1868. Four years later, it was approved as an official agency of the church. Its first secretary was Richard S. Rust.

In one of its first reports, the society stated:

Our missionaries in the South quickly learned that their labors would be fruitless, unless schools should be established, intelligence disseminated and the teachings of the pulpit supplemented by the instruction of the school.[28]

The Freedman's Aid Society had its work cut out for it. One decision which had to be made early was on the location of schools. The need was everywhere but it had to decide upon the most strategic locations. It used one or more of the following criteria in place selection: (1) they should be located at center of population—the density of Negro population was one criterion; (2) they should be located in places where freedmen would cooperate; (3) they should be located in places where schools would be tolerated.

THE WORK OF THE WOMAN'S HOME MISSIONARY SOCIETY

The Woman's Home Missionary Society of the Methodist Episcopal Church was organized in Cincinnati, Ohio on June 8, 1880. It was organized in Trinity Church. Its first president was Mrs. Rutherford Hayes, the wife of the president of the United States.

The General Conference of 1880 approved of the work among Negro women and girls by the women of the church. It should be noted, however, that the women sought participation in the rehabilitation programs of the Freedmen's Aid Society. The women sent a petition to the Board of Managers requesting that women would be included among its Board of Directors. This request was denied because the act of incorporation made males only eligible for membership. Hence, with the General Conference giving tacit approval, the women organized as a counterpart organization to the Freedmen's Aid Society.[29]

Their first attention was directed to the young colored women in the South. Its purpose was expressed in these words:

"to enlist and organize the efforts of Christian Women in behalf of the needy and destitute women of all sections of the country." They began by establishing model homes at various points, chiefly at colleges, where the essentials of good home-making were demonstrated.

In its report to the board of managers in 1885, the Woman's Home Missionary Society stated:

> Our society has four industrial homes associated with the schools of the Freedmen's Aid Society in successful operation. These are at Atlanta, Georgia, Little Rock, Arkansas, Holly Springs, Mississippi, and Orangeburg, South Carolina. . . . These homes are arranged to accommodate sixteen girls.[30]

The oldest of these model homes was Thayer Home in Atlanta, Georgia. It was located on Clark campus. The next in order of establishment was Simpson Home on Claflin campus. The third was E. L. Rust Home on Rust College campus. It was opened on October 1, 1884. The Adeline Smith Home was established on Philander Smith campus on February 25, 1884.

In 1884, the Woman's Home Missionary Society contributed $7,305.61 for maintenance and erection of these homes and small stipends for the missionaries who worked in these homes. In addition, this organization contributed $1,589.76 for scholarships to these girls who lived in the model homes.

These two organizations: The Freedmen's Aid Society and the Woman's Home Missionary Society became co-partners in Christian training for the freedmen in the South. They worked hard to thaw the social iceberg in the Deep South.

EXTANT NEGRO INSTITUTIONS

The Methodist Episcopal Church organized twenty-five institutions for Blacks in the black conferences.[31] At least one school was started in each annual conference. Today, there are twelve of these schools still surviving. In addition, Paine College is now included as a result of the Plan of Union of three branches of Methodism adopted in 1939. Two schools are professional: Gammon Theological Seminary and Meharry Medical College. The Morristown Normal and Industrial College is a junior college. Nine colleges are accredited coeducational institutions. Bennett College has been a college for girls since 1926. These schools represent the result of the prodigious efforts of the Freedmen's Aid Society and The Woman's Home Missionary Society.

Rust College

The oldest of the schools started by the Freedmen's Aid Society now extant is Rust College. It was organized as Shaw University in 1866. It began in Asbury Church. Its first principal was the Reverend A. C. McDonald. In 1868, the Freedmen's Aid Society took full control of this school.

The first outstanding contributor to the school was S. P. Shaw. He donated $10,000 for the erection of the first building. The school was first named in his honor. In 1891, the name was changed to Rust University in honor of the Reverend Richard S. Rust, corresponding secretary of the Freedmen's Aid Society.

Rust College has had eleven presidents during its history. The president today is Dr. W. A. McMillian. He was elected in 1967.

Dillard University

Although Dillard University represents a recent merger, its roots lie in the establishment of Thomson Institute by the Mississippi Mission Conference in 1866. The institute was established to "educate the colored ministers of the Methodist

50

Episcopal Church." The New Orleans University was an outgrowth of the Thomson Institute. It was established in New Orleans in 1873. In 1869, Straight University was founded by the American Missionary Association.

Dillard University represents a merger of New Orleans University, a Methodist institution and Straight University, an American Missionary Association school. It was formally organized on June 6, 1930. This merged institution has been served by four former presidents. The present president is Samuel Cook. He was elected in 1974.

Claflin College

Claflin College was founded in 1869. It represented a merger between the Baker Institute, Charleston, South Carolina and Training school at Camden, South Carolina. The merged school was located in Orangeburg, South Carolina. From its beginning, this school has been closely related to the South Carolina Conference. Its relationship to the conference is unparalleled among the black colleges of the church. The people of the South Carolina Conference bought into ownership from its very beginning. It has received the greatest financial support from this conference than any of the schools from the conferences in which they are located.

Claflin has had six presidents in its history. The Reverend Hubert V. Manning is now president. He has served for twenty-two years.

Clark College

Clark College was organized in the Lloyd Street (Central) Church in Atlanta, Georgia in February, 1872. It started earlier as a primary school in the Summer Hill Section of Atlanta. It was then under the supervision of the Reverend J. W. Lee. In 1869, The Freedmen's Aid Society assumed responsibility for the school. Clark was organized primarily to train ministers.

Clark has had nineteen presidents during its years of existence. The last president, Vivian Henderson, died January 28, 1976. Elias Blake was elected President in 1977.

Bethune Cookman College

Bethune Cookman College is a merger between Cookman Institute located in Jacksonville, Florida, and Daytona Normal, an industrial institute for Negro girls at Daytona Beach, Florida. Cookman Institute was started in 1872 by the Freedmen's Aid Society. It was the oldest institution for higher education for Negroes in Florida.

In 1923, the Cookman Institute merged with the Daytona Normal Institute for girls. The Daytona Normal School was founded by Mrs. Mary McLeod Bethune in 1903. The merged institution became Bethune Cookman College. This merged institution has had only three former presidents. The present president is Dr. Oswald P. Bronson. He was elected in 1975.

Bennett College

Bennett College began in the basement of Saint Matthew Methodist Episcopal Church in Greensboro, North Carolina in 1873 with Mr. W. J. Parker in charge. In 1874, the Freedmen's Aid Society took over supervision of the school.

The school was named in honor of Mr. Lyman Bennett of Troy, New York. He donated $10,000.00 toward the establishment of the school in North Carolina. The North Carolina Conference assisted in the purchase of twenty acres of land.

From 1873 until 1926, Bennett College was coeducational. Three of the black bishops are listed as alumni of the school: Robert E. Jones, Matthew W. Clair, Sr., and Robert N. Brooks.

Bennett College has had ten previous presidents. The president now is Dr. Isaac H. Miller, Jr. He was elected in 1966.

Wiley College

Wiley College was the first school to be established by the Freedmen's Aid Society west of the Mississippi River. It was opened on March 17, 1873. It was named in the honor of Bishop I. W. Wiley. He was the president of the Freedmen's Aid Society at that time.

Including the present president, this college has had eleven presidents. The Reverend Robert Hayes was elected president in 1971.

Meharry Medical College

The Meharry Medical College began as a department of Central Tennessee College in Nashville, Tennessee. It opened in 1876 with nine students. It received its name from the Meharry brothers who were the first donors to the school. In 1915, Meharry Medical College secured its own charter. The president now is Lloyd C. Elam. He was elected in 1968.

Philander Smith College

Philander Smith College began as Walden Seminary on November 2, 1877. It was founded in Wesley Methodist Episcopal Church in Little Rock, Arkansas. From its beginning, it was related to the Little Rock Conference. It became Philander Smith College in 1883. Its name was changed to Philander Smith College because Mrs. Adeline M. Smith of Oak Park, Illinois, gave $17,000.00 in memory of her late husband.

This school has had nine presidents. The Reverend Walter R. Hazzard was elected president in 1969.

Morristown Junior College

The Morristown Junior College was founded in 1881. It began in an old Baptist Church. From its beginning, it has been closely related to the East Tennesee Conference. On its campus, the Woman's Home Missionary Society erected a home for girls in 1890. Including the present president, this school has had nine presidents. The Reverend Raymond White was elected in 1972.

Paine College

Paine College was the exception. It was not started by the Freedmen's Aid Society. It began as a cooperative educational venture between the Colored Methodist Episcopal Church and the Methodist Episcopal Church South in 1882. It was named in memory of Bishop Robert Paine of the Methodist Episcopal Church South. During its history, it has had eleven presidents, only two of which have been black. The first black to be elected was Lucius Pitts in 1971. In 1975, Dr. J. S. Scott, Jr. was elected as the second black president.

Gammon Theological Seminary

Gammon Theological Seminary began as the Bible Department of Clark University. In 1883, it became an independent institution and a school of theology. It was named in honor of Mr. Elijah Gammon from Maine. He and his wife contributed $25,000 toward the training of Negro ministers.

Gammon like all other institutions has had an open door policy. In its bulletin of 1889, these words are found:

> Gammon Theological Seminary offers without distinction of race to students for the Christian Ministry as thorough, extensive and well arranged a course of study as an institution in this country. It is the only distinctively theological school in the South on this broad basis.

Although Gammon Seminary was Methodist operated, it has trained men of all denominations for the Christian ministry. By 1895, it was also interracial in faculty and student body. In 1897, John H. Shillings, a white student, received his Bachelor of Divinity degree from Gammon.

Gammon has had twelve presidents during its existence. The Reverend Major J. Jones was elected president in 1967.

Huston-Tillotson College

A preparatory school began in the St. Paul Church in Dallas, Texas by G. W. Richardson in 1876. Soon after, it was decided that Dallas was not the best location for a conference school.

In September 1878, the Andrew Normal School was relocated in Austin, Texas. It began its instructional work in the Wesley Church.

The first substantial donation was made by Mr. Samuel Huston of Morengo, Iowa. The college was named in honor of this first donor.

For twenty years or more, obstacles impeded the progress of developing a full fledged institution. In 1900, the school became a reality. It has had an eventful history thereafter.

In 1952, Samuel Huston College merged with Tillotson College, an American Missionary Association school. This merged school has had three presidents. In 1965, Dr. King was elected as its third president.

THE ROLE OF BLACK COLLEGES

The black colleges just named have played a significant role in the development of black Methodism. Most ministerial and lay leaders have been nurtured in these institutions. They have always had an open door policy. Some non-Methodists have left these institutions as professing Methodists. Black

Methodist memberships are stronger numerically in states where these colleges are located, with the exceptions of Florida and Arkansas.

Other black Methodist denominations also seem to prosper where they have planted colleges. The predominant black Methodist denomination in North Carolina is the African Methodist Episcopal Zion Church; Livingstone College is located in Salisbury. Similarly, the African Methodist Episcopal Church is the strongest black Methodist group in Georgia. Morris Brown College is located in Atlanta. The Christian Methodist Episcopal Church has Lane College in Jackson, Tennessee. This denomination has strong membership in Tennessee.

Black colleges have served as the custodian of African heritage. An appreciation for black culture has been developed. They have provided remedial instructions for students who have been shortchanged by nurture and not by nature.

WILLIAM HENRY CROGMAN

The first colored teacher to be employed by the Freedmen's Aid Society was William Henry Crogman.[32] He began his teaching career at Claflin College in 1870.

He was born on the Island of Saint Martin, West Indies, on May 5, 1841. Upon the encouragement of an interested friend, he entered Pierce Academy in Massachusetts. He became an honor student at that school.

In 1877, he joined the faculty at Clark College. He was the Professor of Greek and Latin. He served as president of Clark College from 1903–1910.

He served as the superintendent of the Sunday School at Clark for twenty-seven years. He was the secretary of the Board of Trustees at Clark from 1878 until April 26, 1923. He was a delegate to the 1880, 1884, and 1888 General Conference from the Savannah Conference.

He retired on May 10, 1922. The Carnegie Foundation granted him a pension for life. He died on October 16, 1931.

The Humble Beginnings of Some Black Churches

Within black Methodism are some churches which have significance beyond the location of the particular church. Included in this chapter are some churches in which colleges and conferences were organized. Others are included because of their historical significance or because they were the first black churches in particular sections of the country.

THE ZOAR CHURCH, PHILADELPHIA, PENNSYLVANIA

The most authentic record available shows that Zoar is the oldest continuing black United Methodist church in the United States. It began as the African Zoar Society in the section of Philadephia called Campington. It started in a butcher shop.

In 1794, the first lot was purchased and the first edifice was erected. In his journal, Frances Asbury made this entry: "On August 4, 1796, I was called upon by the African Society in Campington to open their new church."

Many of the early leaders of historic Methodism graced this pulpit. Among the many, the following are cited: Thomas Coke, William Calbert, Henry Boehm, a German Methodist, and Harry Hoosier.

In the early years of existence, the church was served by black local preachers. The following ministers served the church from 1864–1900:

Issac Henson	1864–1865	John H. Pearce	1866–1867
J. D. Elbert	1868–1869	Hooper Jolly	1870–1871
W. G. Parker	1872–1875	J. G. Dennis	1876
W. C. Dickerson	1877–1879	W. H. Caffey	1880–1881
W. F. Butler	1882	W. H. Thomas	1883
A. R. Shockley	1884–1885	J. H. Reddick	1886–1889
W. H. Thomas	1890	J. L. Cole	1891–1892
T. H. Johnson	1893	T. S. Als	1894
J. A. Richardson	1895–1898	H. A. Monroe	1899–1900

In 1900, this church had a membership of 517.

The second oldest continuing congregation in black Methodism is the Sharp Street Church. On May 15, 1802, James Carey conveyed to the Trustees of the African Academy a deed for a lot on the west side of Sharp Street running back a depth of one hundred feet. The lot was 50 by 100 feet. The deed made the following provision:

> For the preaching of God's word, for self perpetuation of the trustees, the purchase price of $1,450. The lot of ground and buildings shall be for the use and benefit and serve as a school for the education of black children of every persuasion and for the benefits of Africans of Baltimore belonging to and in communion with the Society of Christians known by the name of the Methodist Episcopal Church in America.

On May 30, 1811, for the price of $1,000, Jacob Sinclair conveyed another lot, behind the first lot. It was 50 by 30 feet, and on it was a three-story building.

In order to purchase the second lot, a mortgage was given on the first lot. Of the nine Blacks who executed the paper, two were able to sign their own names.

In 1860, the "Old Church" was remodeled. In 1864, the Washington Conference was organized in this church. Two years later, the Central Biblical Institute (Morgan College) was started in this church.

From 1864 to 1900, the following men served this historic church:

John N. Mars	1864	J. H. Harper	1865
J. H. Price	1866–1867	W. W. Cook	1868
James Peck	1869–1870	R. H. Robinson	1871–1872
P. G. Walker	1873–1875	R. H. Robinson	1876
C. S. Keys	1877–1879	John A. Holmes	1880–1882
J. W. Dansberry	1883–1885	E. W. S. Peck	1886–1888
J. H. Dailey	1889	G. G. Griffin	1890
W. M. Carroll	1891–1895	D. W. Hayes	1896–1899
Alfred Young	1900		

In 1900, this church had a membership of 1,261 full members.

Asbury Church, Washington, D. C.

The Foundry United Methodist is the Mother of Asbury Church. The Foundry Church had Negro members since 1814. They were put in classes and led by white brethren of the church. In 1817, there were 172 white and 118 Negro members. By 1827, the Negro membership of Foundry Church had increased to 176.

On September 27, 1833, Eli Neugent was granted exhorter's license. In 1840, he received deacon's orders.

The black membership in Foundry grew so rapidly that it was believed that the Negroes could best be served by becoming a separate congregation. In 1836, the black members were organized in a separate congregation.

A site was selected at the corner of 11th and K Street, northwest. A frame building was erected in 1836. The Negro congregation was named in honor of Bishop Francis Asbury.

The following are charter members of Asbury Church:

Praeter Hutt	Mary Hutt
Eli Neugent	Charlotte Neugent
Jenny Bateman	Isaiah Bateman
Moses Dick	Caroline Mason
Sarah Fletcher	William A. Wilson
John Brent	Moses Smallwood
Kathy Sims	Martha Garner
Betsy Cohelery	Sarah D. Height
Mary Sims	Lonnie Johnson
William Ingram	George Ingram
John Cartright	Robert Bell

The following men served as the pastors of this historic church:

James Peck	1864	Richard Bell	1865–1866
Ceasar Johnson	1867–1868	R. H. Robinson	1869–1870
W. W. Foreman	1871–1872	Benjamin Brown	1873
J. Thomas	1874–1876	J. D. S. Hall	1877
E. W. S. Peck	1878–1880	N. M. Carroll	1881–1883
R. A. Reed	1884–1886	J. H. Dailey	1887
G. G. Griffin	1888–1889	J. W. E. Bowen, Sr.	1890–1892
D. W. Hayes	1893–1895	I. L. Thomas	1896–1900

In 1900, this church reported 750 full church members.

OLD BETHEL CHURCH, CHARLESTON, SOUTH CAROLINA

The Old Bethel Church in Charleston is perhaps the oldest Negro United Methodist church in South Carolina.

When W. Lewis was sent down by Bishop Osmon Baker as a Missionary in the South in 1862, he found a nucleus of black Methodists in Charleston.

By now the Negro members had been given Old Bethel Church. In 1853, this church was moved across the street from its former location. It has been a continuing congregation since that date. It was supplied by local preachers for many years.

From 1864 to 1900, the following ministers have served this congregation:

Alonzo Webster and W. O. Weston	1868	T. W. Lewis (white)	1869–1873
G. Weston	1874	J. A. Sasportas	1875–1877
Daniel Minus	1878–1879	E. C. Brown	1880–1882
H. Cardoza	1883–1885	J. A. Brown	1886–1887
B. F. Witherspoon	1888–1891	C. C. Jacobs	1892–1895
J. H. Johnson	1896–1897	J. B. Middleton	1898
J. A. Brown	1899–1900		

In 1900, Old Bethel had a membership of 315 full members.

Wesley Church, Little Rock, Arkansas

In 1853, the black members of the white Methodist Episcopal Church South in Little Rock outgrew the space provided for them in the white church. A frame building was erected for them near Eight and Broadway Streets. It was named Wesley Chapel.

Although the black congregation was separate, it was still governed by the white church. Local preachers were provided for them.

After Emancipation, the Reverend William A. Andrews, a local preacher, encouraged the black members to unite with the Methodist Episcopal Church.

This church was transferred into the Missouri-Arkansas Conference. It reported a membership of sixty-three full members.

In 1877, Walden Seminary (now Philander Smith College) was organized in this church. It continued to hold classes here until 1879.

In 1883, the pastor, W. O. Emory and his presiding elder, Isaac G. Pollard, purchased the present site and erected the first brick structure. The following pastors have served this congregation:

W. A. Andrews	1864–1865	Lewis H. Carthart	1866
S. Alexander	1867–1869	T. Harden	1870
H. L. Miller	1871	W. H. Brown	1872
E. W. S. Peck	1873	W. H. Crawford	1874–1875
George Sam	1876	A. J. Phillips	1877
Alexander Scott	1878	J. G. Thompson	1879–1880
W. O. Emory	1881–1883	W. H. McCallister	1884–1885
W. H. Crawford	1886	Seth Neal	1887
G. W. Lacy	1888	A. J. Fletcher	1889–1890
J. E. Toombs	1891–1892	W. O. Emory	1893–1895
R. R. Duncan	1896–1897	J. C. Sherrill	1898
G. W. Johnson	1899–1900		

This church had a membership of 405 in 1900.

TINDLEY TEMPLE, PHILADELPHIA, PENNSYLVANIA

The Tindley Temple Church grew out of Zoar Church. Some members became dissatisfied and left the mother church to establish their own church. Before the small group was able to erect their church, they worshipped in homes.

In 1864, the little congregation erected its first church. It was erected at the corner of Eight and Bainbridge Streets. It seated fifty persons. The name of the first church was John Wesley.

In 1882, Bishop Matthew Simpson assisted in the securing of a new location. It secured the Old Bainbridge Street Church at the corner of Bainbridge and Florida Streets (now Marvine Street). The name of the church was changed to the Bainbridge Street Methodist Episcopal Church.

In 1906, the Westminister Presbyterian Church was purchased. It was located at the southwest corner of Broad and Fitzwater Streets. Again the church changed its name to East Calvary Methodist Episcopal Church. In 1924, for the rich ministry of the Reverend Charles A. Tindley, the church's name was changed to Tindley Temple.

The following persons were charter members of the first congregation: Henry Simm, Peter Wise, George Curtis, John Taylor, Mary and Harriet Norris. Simm was a local preacher.

The Delaware Conference was organized in John Wesley (Tindley Temple) on July 29, 1864.

The following pastors have served this church from 1865–1900:

Abraham Brown	1865	To be supplied	1866
J. S. Mantuff	1867	S. P. Whittington	1868
Soloman Cooper	1869	S. Johns	1870–1871
B. Gibbes	1872	S. P. Marshall	1873
Isaiah Broughton	1874–1875	J. H. Pearce	1876–1877
Peter Burrows	1878–1879	W. Morris	1880–1881
B. W. Allen	1882	J. W. Stevenson	1883
Hooper Jolly	1884–1885	L. Y. Cox	1886–1887
E. E. Parker	1888–1890	J. H. Reddick	1891–1892
W. H. Caffe	1893–1894	Pezavia O'Connell	1895–1898
J. H. Nutter	1899–1901		

Tindley Temple had a membership of 389 in 1900.

WESLEY CHURCH, NEW ORLEANS, LOUISIANA

Perhaps the oldest church west of the Mississippi River is the Wesley Church, New Orleans, Louisiana. It was started in 1838. In 1842, it appeared as a black appointment in the Louisiana Conference. It reported 600 members in 1843. In 1858, the church was closed in compliance with a city ordinance. In 1864, John Paul Newman reorganized the church.

The Mississippi Mission Conference was organized in this church by Bishop Thomson on December 25, 1865. The following ministers have served this church from 1865–1900:

Anthony Ross	1865–1868	To be supplied	1869–1870
J. Heywood	1871–1873	J. Gould	1874–1876
J. M. Vance	1877	Marcus Dale	1878–1879
Emperor Williams	1880	Samuel Davage	1881–1883
Marcus Dale	1884	T. Johnson	1885
Marcus Dale	1886	F. T. Chinn	1887–1891
T. Johnson	1892–1895	Pierre Landry	1897–1900

In 1900, the Wesley Church had 453 full members.

WESLEY CHAPEL, AUSTIN, TEXAS

On March 4, 1865, the Reverend Joseph Welch presided over a meeting at which the Wesley Church was founded. It was held in the basement of the Old Tenth Street Methodist Episcopal Church South.

On the next day, the first quarterly conference was held. The following men were elected as trustees: Milton Wright, Thomas Merridy, Tom King, Simon Dedrick, Grant Woods, Harry Shelby, Samuel Hamilton, and Reverend Isaac Wright.

When the church was officially opened, 275 members united with the church. They became the charter members of this church.

The first building was erected under the leadership of the Reverend B. F. Williams in 1874. It was located on the corner of Fourth Street and Congress Avenue. Its dimensions were 40 by 60 feet.

The West Texas Conference began in this church. It was organized in Wesley Church on January 22, 1874.

In 1882, the new church at the corner of Ninth and Neches Street was erected. Its estimated cost was $22,000.

When Samuel Houston College was moved from Dallas to Austin, it was located in this church. For many years, classes were held in this church.

In 1928, a new location was secured for the church on Hackberry and St. Bernard Streets. It was purchased during the pastorate of L. H. Robinson. The new church was built during the pastorate of the Reverend W. L. Turner.

The following pastors have served this church from 1865–1900:

Isaac Wright	1865–1868	B. F. Williams	1868–1870
E. Dibble	1871	David Gregory	1872–1873
Samuel Gates	1874–1876	C. L. Madison	1877
David Gregory	1878–1879	C. L. Madison	1879–1880
A. R. Norris	1881	Harry Swann	1882–1885
P. Morgan	1886	Mack Henson	1887–1889
P. M. Carmichael	1890–1891	C. L. Madison	1892–1893
Andrew Foster	1894	John T. Gibbons	1895
Andrew Foster	1896–1897	G. R. Bryant	1898–1900

This church had a membership of 659 full members in 1900.

TRINITY CHURCH, HOUSTON, TEXAS

On Thursday, March 5, 1865, a meeting was held in the home of Richard Brook, north of Buffalo Bayou, for the purpose of organizing a Methodist Episcopal Church.

The meeting was presided over by the Reverend David Dibble. This small group organized and became Trinity

Church. For two years this group met in Reverend Dibble's kitchen for worship.

In 1867, a resolution was passed to erect a church. The following resolution was adopted:

> Resolved that, we, the ex-slaves living in the First Ward of Houston, build a church for public worship; said building to be 25 feet by 150 feet, cost $500.00 and bear the name of Trinity Methodist Episcopal Church.

Twenty-five persons subscribed $300.00. They built the first Negro church in Houston, Texas.

The Texas Conference was organized in this church in 1867. The following pastors have served this church from 1865 to 1900:

David Dibble	1865–1867	Samuel Osborn	1868
David Gregory	1869–1870	J. Shackelford	1871–1872
Spencer Hardwell	1873–1875	J. Shackelford	1876
J. L. Loggins	1877–1878	P. Douglass	1879–1880
I. B. Scott	1881–1882	W. H. Logan	1883–1885
Mack Henson	1886	William Wesley	1887
C. C. Minnegan	1888–1890	V. M. Cole	1891–1893
Wade Hamilton	1894–1895	Freedman Parker	1896
Wade Hamilton	1897	L. L. Blackney	1898–1899
W. H. Logan	1900		

In 1900, Trinity Church had 382 full members.

Clark Memorial Church, Nashville, Tennessee

In 1865, the Methodist Episcopal Church began its missionary work in Nashville, Tennessee. It purchased a lot and a building which had formerly belonged to the Methodist Episcopal Church South. Its original name was Andrew Chapel.

The first church was constructed in 1847. During the Civil War, this house was used as a barracks for the Union Army.

During the time that it was a Negro church in the Methodist Episcopal Church South, the following bishops had been members: Bishop Evans Tyree, Charles S. Smith of the African Methodist Episcopal Church, John J. Moreland of the African Methodist Episcopal Zion Church. Three men who were members of this church became bishops in the Colored Methodist Episcopal Church: Charles Phillips, Elias Cottrell, and George Stewart.

When the Missionary Society purchased this church, it was named Clark Chapel in honor of Bishop D. W. Clark, President of the Freedmen's Aid Society. It was located on Franklin Street, Third and Fourth Avenue South.

By August 27, 1868, this enterprising congregation had paid $15,000 to the Missionary Society for the property. In transferring the title to this group, this was placed in the deeds: "Property is to be used for divine worship and a school for the education of Negro youth."

The original trustees were Randell Brown, Alfred Minabee, Eli Polk, Samuel Ewing, Henry Tagrin, Madison Trimbelle, Squire Faine, Ephraim Prickett, and Wiley Ramsey. Randell Brown and Alfred Minabee were free Negroes and could read and write. In addition, Randall Brown was an incorporator of the Mount Ararat Cemetery in 1861, the first corporation formed and operated by Negroes in Tennessee.

The Central Tennessee College (later Walden College) was organized in this church in 1866. Meharry Medical College was originally a department of this college.

The following men have served as pastors of this church from 1865–1900:

John Seay	1866	W. B. Crichlow	1866–1867
John Braden	1867–1868	William Butler	1868–1869
Calvin Pickett	1869–1870	James Pickett	1870–1872
J. C. Thompson	1872–1874	William Butler	1874–1876
C. S. Smith	1876–1877	C. W. Wood	1878
D. W. Hayes	1879–1881	L. M. Haygood	1881–1884
Andrew Phillips	1884–1886	J. B. Bradford	1886–1888
H. W. White	1888–1892	C. B. Wilson	1892–1897
G. W. Zeigler	1897–1900		

In 1900, Clark Memorial Church had 450 full members.

Asbury Church, Canton, Mississippi

Asbury Church is one of the oldest churches in the Mississippi Conference. In 1865, Mr. Redrick Thomas and Mr. Caliph Whiting, with their families and others, organized the Asbury Church. It was first located on East Academy Street.

On January 7, 1869, the Mississippi Conference was organized in Asbury Church. It was the second conference to develop out of the Mississippi Mission Conference.

From 1865 until 1900, the following pastors served this church:

To be supplied	1865–1866	A. Handy	1867–1870
E. Scarborough	1871–1873	J. A. Moore	1874
E. Graves	1875	A. Handy	1876–1878
James Parks	1879–1881	D. D. Goodwin	1882
A. K. Davis	1883–1887	P. H. Davis	1888–1891
J. C. Hibbler	1892	S. J. Woods	1893
R. P. Thirkeld	1894–1896	Wilson Toole	1897–1900

In 1900, the Asbury Church had 200 full members.

Central Church, Atlanta, Georgia

The Central United Methodist Church was organized by the Reverend J. W. Lee in 1866. Its first name was Clark Chapel in honor of Bishop D. W. Clark. By 1870, the name was changed to Lloyd Street Church. It was first located on Fraser Street in the Summerhill section of Atlanta. One of the first trustees of this church was a white man named Kimball, the founder of Kimball House. Some of the charter members were: John Leake and family, I. H. Alexander, Adeline Singleton, George Payne, and George Glenn. In 1876, the church was sold to colored members for a very modest sum. It was located on Central Street near Hunter Street. The church was named Central Church later.

In 1872, Clark College had its humble beginning in

Central Church. In 1896, the Atlanta Conference was also organized in this church. The following pastors have served this church from 1866 to 1900:

J. W. Lee	1866	George Kendall	1867
Joseph Sans	1868–1869	J. H. Knowles	1870–1871
Moses Robinson	1872–1873	W. B. Osborne	1874
I. J. Lansing	1875	G. Standing	1876–1879
J. B. L. Williams	1880	C. O. Fisher	1881–1883
A. P. Melton	1884–1885	George Standing	1886–1887
M. B. C. Mason	1888–1891	G. W. Arnold	1892–1895
G. J. Harris	1896	R. J. Adams	1897–1898
J. A. Rush	1899–1900		

Central Church had 860 members in 1900.

SAINT MATTHEW CHURCH, GREENSBORO, NORTH CAROLINA

The Saint Matthew Church was organized in Greensboro, North Carolina in 1866 by the Reverend Matthew Alston. It is the oldest Negro church in Greensboro, North Carolina.

Among the first members of the church were D. B. Yancy, W. S. Garrett, J. P. Morris, R. B. Williams, Aaron Mendenhall, J. D. Chavis, Thomas D. Moore, Rufus M. McKensie, J. L. Bullock, and W. B. Windsor.

The first church was built of handmade bricks, and many members contributed services to the erection of their church.

In 1873, Bennett College had its beginnings in the unplastered basement of Saint Matthew's Church. It held classes here for several months.

The following ministers served this church from 1866 to 1900:

Matthew Alston	1866–1868	H. F. Pope	1869–1870
S. L. Rogers	1871	W. W. Morgan	1872
M. G. Croon	1873–1875	E. Moten	1876
J. E. Champion	1877–1878	E. Walker	1879–1880
To be supplied	1881	W. H. Golar	1882–1883
H. M. Murphy	1884–1885	L. B. Gibson	1886
R. C. Campbell	1887–1888	Pezavia O'Connell	1889–1891
R. A. Cottingham	1892	J. A. Rush	1893–1894
M. M. Jones	1895–1897		
S. A. Peeler	1898–1900		

Saint Matthew Church had a membership of 456 members in 1900.

ASBURY CHURCH, HOLLY SPRINGS, MISSISSIPPI

In 1866, Asbury Church was organized by the Reverend A. C. McDonald, a white missionary from Iowa and the Reverend Moses Adam, an ex-slave. It was first located on Walthall Street. It was named in memory of Francis Asbury. Later it was moved to College Avenue.

In this church, Rust College was founded. Classes were begun in this church in late 1866. On February 5, 1891, the Upper Mississippi Conference was organized in Asbury Church. The following men served as pastors of this church from 1866 to 1900:

Moses Adams	1866	A. William	1867–1868
Moses Adams	1869	C. W. Fitzburgh	1870
S. H. Scott	1871–1874	H. R. Revels	1875
Peter Blue	1876	J. M. Shumpert	1877–1879
W. H. H. Gallion	1880	A. K. Davis	1881
S. A. Cowan	1882–1884	A. M. Trotter	1885–1887
J. H. McCallister	1888	B. H. S. Ferguson	1889–1892
J. L. Wilson	1893–1895	G. G. Logan	1896
W. C. Clay	1897–1900		

By 1900, Asbury Church had a membership of 260 full members.

THE SAINT MARK CHURCH, NEW YORK, NEW YORK

The Saint Mark Methodist Church claims the honor of being the oldest continuing United Methodist black fellowship in New York. An early effort had been made by the City Mission and Church Extension Society to establish a Methodist Episcopal church for Negroes in the city of New York.

A lot was purchased on Attorney Street, but the establishment of a Negro congregation failed.

In 1871. the African Methodist Episcopal Zion Conference convened in Mother Zion Church. The entertaining pastor was the Reverend William F. Butler. A feud developed between him and Bishop Hood. It resulted in Pastor Butler withdrawing from this denomination.

Without denominational affiliation, the Reverend Butler decided to organize a Methodist Episcopal church for Negroes in New York City. He made contact with Bishop Gilbert Haven. He found immediate favor from the bishop. Soon the bishop sent him a letter of introduction to be given to Mr. William B. Cornell, President of the City Mission and Church Extension. Shortly afterwards, Mr. Cornell approved the application for aid and pledged support to the Reverend Butler's efforts to establish a Negro church.

The City Mission and Church Extension Society employed the Reverend Butler for three years. It provided a salary and parsonage for him.

After a search was made for a location, one was found in Washington Hall on Broadway in the Times Square area. The name of the new church was to be the Saint Mark Methodist Episcopal Church. Credit is given to Mrs. Maggie Dickinson for suggesting the name.

On July 1, 1871, the church was opened. The following were charter members: Mrs. Jemima Belkizer, Mr. and Mrs. Daniel Ladlow, Mrs. Downs, Mrs. Gomez, Mrs. Houston, Mrs. Wallace, and Mrs. Maggie Dickinson. The following pastors have served this church from 1871–1900:

William F. Butler	1871–1875	E. W. S. Peck	1875–1878
Richard A. Read	1878–1881	William P. Ryder	1881–1884
John A. Holmes	1884–1887	Henry A. Monroe	1887–1892
Ernest Lyon	1892–1897	William H. Brooks	1897–1923

By the turn of the century, Saint Mark Church had a membership of 450 full members.

WESLEY CHURCH, LOS ANGELES, CALIFORNIA

About a century ago, the West was referred to as "Methodism's Promised Land." According to Christian F. F. Reisner, much of the West was a mission country as late as 1883.

Among the early missionary efforts of the Methodist Episcopal Church was the establishment of Wesley Methodist Episcopal Church for Negroes. In 1888, Wesley Church started as a Negro mission in Los Angeles, California. It is perhaps the oldest black Methodist church in Southern California. It was started by F. H. Tubbs.

The following pastors served this church from 1888 to 1900:

A. H. Tubbs	1888–1890		
David Macher	1891–1892	S. W. Wawkins	1893–1899
F. S. Donohoo	1900		

In 1900, the Wesley Church had a membership of 202 full members.

Black Church Membership in 1900

By 1900, the 18 Negro conferences had 1,705 ministers in full connection, 3,398 churches with an aggregate church membership of 239,274.

Of this total membership, 174,950 members were living in the South. There were 2,301 organized congregations in the South in that year.

In 1900, farming was the chief occupation for Negroes. According to Weatherford, 53.7 percent of all Negro workers were engaged in farming at the turn of the century.[33] In addition, 92 percent of the Negroes lived in the South.

Of this total number living in the South, 136,635 lived in states where cotton was the principal product. There were 1,787 churches in these states. Many were located on plantations or in the open country. Only 33 churches were located

71

in population centers of 10,000 or more. These churches had a combined membership of 10,571, most were mission stations.

The Changing Social Conditions in the South and Their Effect Upon Inclusive Conference Membership

In 1864, the General Conference authorized the organization of Mission Conferences in the South. At the time of organization, all conferences were inclusive except Kentucky. The 1868 General Conference authorized the organization of a colored conference in Kentucky.

Soon after the war, the social conditions began to change in the South, which had an effect upon the church. In 1875, Congress passed legislation guaranteeing the Negroes equal access to hotels, restaurants and other public accommodations. The Supreme Court declared the law unconstitutional in its ruling on the civil rights cases in 1883. By that time almost all civil rights legislation had been invalidated or vitiated by the Compromise of 1877, which brought the withdrawal of federal troops from the South. In the absence of federal troops, white supremacists felt free to abridge the civil rights of Negroes under Jim Crow Laws and white terror. The blacks again became totally disenfranchised and segregated.

In 1896, the Supreme Court struck a death blow to social interaction. In the case of Plessy vs. Ferguson, racial segregation received official sanction in the verdict of the court on May 18, 1896. Justice Henry B. Brown wrote the eight man majority and ruled that "separate but equal public facilities were constitutional." This action made it almost impossible to continue with integrated conferences in the South.

In anticipation of this decision, the General Conference authorized the bishops to divide the conferences in the South when mutually agreeable to the majority of both groups and approved by the presiding bishop in 1876. By 1900, all conferences had been divided into white and colored conferences.

CHAPTER V

Black Conferences Under White Leadership, 1901-1919

Prior to 1900, conferences in the South were inclusive. They were supervised by white bishops. Although the bishop was removed by social barriers and geography, he had an inter-racial cabinet. Some white presiding elders kept the bishops informed about the status of the conference.

By 1900, all conferences were Negro conferences. No longer did the bishop have white presiding elders in his cabinet. He relied upon the advice of a Negro presiding elder to play the role of an informant. The role became institutionalized. The person so chosen became a "sub-bishop" in Negro conferences. These men became very powerful and remained in this role for an indefinite period, even after Negroes were elected to the episcopacy.

Changing Attitudes Regarding the Election of Black Elders As Bishops

In 1872, Negro leaders presented a resolution to the General Conference requesting that a man of African descent would be elected to the episcopacy. The colored delegate, James Lynch of Mississippi, read the resolution.

The General Conference did not approve the resolution. This conference did adopt however the following resolution:

73

There is nothing in race, color or former condition, that is a bar to an election to the episcopacy, the true course being for us to elect only such persons as are by their pre-eminent piety, endowments, culture, general fitness and acceptability best qualified to fill the office . . . Being of African descent does not prevent membership with white men in annual conference nor ordination at the same altars, nor appointment or eligibility to the highest office.[1]

With the adoption of this resolution, "colored" was stricken from the Discipline, making all ministers eligible for leadership roles based upon *qualifications* and *acceptability*.

In 1896, the black delegates discovered a qualified black elder for the highest office. The Reverend John Wesley Bowen, Sr., of the Washington Conference, was the choice of black delegates. He was the first Negro to earn a Ph.D. from Boston University. He had served in the parish ministry. He was professor of Historical Theology at Gammon Seminary.

On the first ballot, Dr. Bowen received the highest number of votes cast. He received 145.[2] The runner-up, C. C. McCabe, received 141. On the second ballot he received 173 votes but dropped to second place.

Although no bishop was elected until the fifteenth ballot, it was evident the day had not arrived to elect a black man to the episcopacy.

After this General Conference, Negro leaders changed their view. No longer did they request that a black man would be elected to serve the black conferences. Hereafter, the General Conferences were flooded with petitions to elect a black man as a general superintendent.

Women Admitted to the General Conference

The admission of women to the General Conference was a long and hard struggle. Luccock called it the "Thirty Years War" in the Methodist Episcopal Church. Laymen were admitted in 1872, but women were denied the right.

In 1888, five women were elected by annual conferences as delegates to the General Conference. They were denied admission. Among them was Francis Willard. She had served as president of her alma mater. She had served also as president of the Temperance Movement. Still she did not qualify for admission to this General Conference.

In 1896, the bishops of the church expressed the view of the fathers regarding the role of women in the general church. A constitutional amendment was necessary to admit women to the General Conference. In the Episcopal Address, the bishops said:

> We commend that form to you early . . . believing that its adoption by a two-thirds vote of this General Conference after such amendments as you may think wise and by a three-fourths vote of the Annual Conference would be a great advantage of the Church.[3]

In 1900, a constitutional amendment was approved. Women were seated for the first time in the 1904 General Conference.

The black conferences refused to elect black women for several quadrennia. In 1904, only one black woman was elected as a delegate to the General Conference. The Little Rock Conference honored itself by electing Mrs. Annie T. Strickland of Little Rock. She was a teacher in the public school system. In 1908, only one woman delegate was elected by the Negro conferences. The Texas Conference elected Mrs. Rosa Simpson.

The 1912 General Conference

In the episcopal address, the bishops had this to say about the Negro conferences:

> On grounds of expediency and it may as well be said, by mutual preference, in view of all conditions our Negro members have their separate Annual Conferences and local church organizations.[4]

The address urged this General Conference to develop a plan of action that would provide better supervision of the colored work.

A special committee was raised by the General Conference to "look into the needs as to the episcopal supervision and condition of growth of our 325,000 colored members."

The committee reported back to the General Conference within a week. It recommended that the area system would be devised in the church. Bishops would be assigned to areas for presidential and residential supervision for a quadrennium.

The area system had been recommended before. On May 10, 1856, Edward Thomson of the North Ohio Conference made a similar recommendation. It was laid on the table. The press had urged the creation of this system since the turn of the century. Laymen were strong supporters of the area system. They gave two reasons: (1) The cities needed closer and continuing supervision; (2) The bishops previously had to "scatter too much." The need was not for "more bishops but more bishop."

The resolution was approved. It was a compromise measure. It was designed to continue the general superintendency but at the same time to provide closer supervision for the conferences. The bishops were now required to live in the boundary of their areas. The General Conference by adoption of this resolution provided a better ministry for its Negro constituency, but the whole church gained by it as well.

The Negro Members Take a Second Look at the Methodist Episcopal Church

The Negro had been attracted to the Methodist Episcopal Church because of its stand on slavery and its evangelistic appeal. They now began to ask themselves the question: Is the Methodist Episcopal Church genuine? Is the church for real?

The Negro leaders came to realize painfully that electing a black minister to the general superintendency was not on the horizon. They noted also the rapid growth among the independent black Methodist bodies. Their aggregate membership remained around the 300,000 mark.

Three views were enunciated: (1) withdraw from the Church and become another independent Methodist body; (2) remain in the church; (3) invite the independent black Methodist bodies to unite with the Methodist Episcopal Church.

A strong exponent of the first view was Daniel W. Shaw of the Washington Conference.[5] He gave the following reasons: (1) Negroes were an impediment to organic union between the Methodist Episcopal Church and the Methodist Episcopal Church South; (2) membership in the black churches was not increasing, due to lack of black episcopal leadership; (3) the black Methodist churches were deprived of worship experiences inherent in their cultural patterns because they had to use the ritual of the church. Other black denominations made their own ritual to satisfy their basic needs.

Included in his Plan of Separation were the following articles of agreement: (1) church and school property would be turned over to the Negroes in fee simple title; (2) the Methodist Episcopal Church would provide an annual stipend of $120,000, reducible at the rate of $10,000 per quadrennium until the sum be reduced to $50,000; (3) the sum of $50,000 would be permanent or reducible only on the motion of the recipient or on a ratio as suggested above; (4) the new Negro Methodist Church would maintain a fraternal relation with the mother church. This view received good publicity in the press. It was a minority view among the Negro conferences. Conferences passed resolution condemning the plan. On January 20, 1912, the Upper Mississippi Conference adopted the following resolution:

Be it resolved, that we, the members of the Upper Mississippi Conference do hereby re-affirm our allegiance to the Old Church and believe such a course to be unwise and disastrous to the future spiritual and moral development of our people.[6]

The second view was the majority view. By remaining in the Church, it was believed that the Negro membership could serve as a "leaven." By so doing, they could become gadflies to sensitize the "seared" conscience of white Methodists. In support of this view, Sylvester H. Norwood wrote:

We colored members in the Methodist Episcopal Church have an object in view—the securing of equal rights where we are. The bishopric and other positions are incidental to this principle.[7]

The third view was ecumenical. It was described by J. P. Morris of the North Carolina Conference as "Ideal Methodism." All branches of Methodism should be united in one church. On May 12, 1908, Griffin G. Logan of the Upper Mississippi Conference presented a resolution to the General Conference. He advocated cooperation with the black Independent Methodist branches. This resolution was adopted by the General Conference. It was believed that harmonious cooperation would lead ultimately to organic union.

The Effect of Negro Migration Upon the Church

In 1890, ninety-two percent of the Negroes lived in the South. Even in 1910, ninety-one percent of the Negroes lived in the South.[8] At the end of World War I, most Negroes were concentrated in the rural areas.

During the First World War, Negroes began to leave the South. Due to the shortage of laborers in the North, agents went South to recruit laborers. With certain incentives from these agents and the economic plight of the Negroes in the

South, they were easily persuaded to leave the cotton plantations.

There were social causes for the large migration of Negroes to the North. Injustice in the courts, denial of suffrage, discrimination in public conveyances, and inequities in the educational system were among the social causes.

In addition, there was a growing conflict between the Negroes and the functional illiterates among the white race. Both groups became unfriendly competitors as they tried to eke out a living in the South. In speaking of this fact, Weatherford made the following comment:

> Racial antipathies are by no means as common between Negroes and socially secure whites as between Negroes and whites who are precariously situated socially.[9]

The migration of the Negroes affected the church membership of the Methodist Episcopal Church. Many of these people did not unite with the Methodist Episcopal churches in the North. They found a more kindred spirit among the sect type church or independent black Methodist bodies.

The two states which showed the greatest decline in church membership were Mississippi and South Carolina. The Upper Mississippi Conference and the Mississippi Conference reported a combined membership of 45,573 in 1910. By 1918, the membership had declined to 39,461 members, an almost sixteen percent decline. In 1910, the South Carolina Conference reported 55,707 black Methodists, the largest among Negro conferences. By 1918, its membership had declined to 49,830 or approximately twelve percent.

CHAPTER VI

Selected Black Conferences Under Black Leadership, 1920-1939

In 1920, a new era began in the Methodist Episcopal Church. It was significant indeed for black Methodists. It was the achievement of a proximate goal. The door was opened for blacks to enter the episcopacy.

The General Conference convened this year in Des Moines, Iowa. One of the early decisions made was to elect Blacks to the episcopacy.

On May 3, 1920, W. W. Lucas, Ministerial Delegate from the Mississippi Conference, presented the following resolution:

> Whereas, it is becoming increasingly difficult for white bishops to adequately minister to black people because of conditions over which neither they nor we have control, and whereas, a great church like ours representing various racial groups within its fold, the most complete and efficient supervision in order to conserve the best interests of the Kingdom.
>
> Therefore, resolve that we order a commission consisting of one minister and one layman from each episcopal area to be appointed by the bishops to inquire into the needs of this group from the 80 Negro delegates here from the colored conferences . . . report back to the General Con-

ference not later than Friday of this week, their findings
and make such recommendations as their judgment will
give some episcopal leadership of their own race.[1]

Instead of creating another commission, the General
Conference voted to refer to the Committee on Episcopacy.
On May 5, 1920, the Committee on Episcopacy made
its report to the General Conference. It recommended:

(1) That this General Conference would elect two Negro
     Superintendents, and
(2) That these Negro General Superintendents would be
     elected on a separate ballot.[2]

In making the closing remarks, Chairman Downey said,
"It is time to stop resolving and get into the realm of achievement." The report was adopted as "few reports had been
adopted."

The Election and Consecration of
Two Negro General Superintendents

The first order of the day for May 19 was the election of
two Negro general superintendents. On the first ballot, Robert
Elijah Jones, North Carolina Conference, was elected as the
first black general superintendent in the Methodist Episcopal
Church. Bishop-elect Jones was escorted to the platform by
Bishops McDowell and Thirkfield.
On May 20, 1920, Matthew Wesley Clair, Sr., Washing-
ton Conference, was elected as a general superintendent in
the Church. He was escorted to the platform by Bishops
McDowell and Bristol.

On May 23, 1920, the consecration services were held
for all bishops elected. Bishop-elect Jones was consecrated by
Bishops Wilson and Nuelson with Matthew Dogan, Texas

Conference and R. W. Winchester, North Carolina Conference, participating in the "laying on of hands." The consecrators for Bishop-elect Clair, Sr., were Bishops Anderson and McDowell. The Reverend Ernest S. Williams and Stewart H. Brown of the Washington Conference, participated in the ritual of consecration.

Assignment of Black General Superintendents

On May 25, 1920, the Committee on Episcopacy recommended and the conference approved of the assignments. Bishop Robert E. Jones was assigned to the New Orleans Area for residential and presidential supervision. His area was composed of the following Negro conferences: Central Alabama, Louisiana, Mississippi, Texas, Upper Mississippi, and West Texas. Bishop M. W. Clair, Sr. was assigned to the Monrovia Area.[3]

Episcopal Supervision of Other Black Conferences

The other thirteen black conferences were distributed to other episcopal areas under white bishops. In the Chattanooga Area were placed the East Tennessee, Tennessee and the North Carolina Conferences. The Atlanta, Florida, Savannah, South Carolina, and the South Florida Mission were assigned to the Atlanta Area. The Delaware Conference was placed in the Philadelphia Area, and the Washington Conference was assigned to the Washington Area. The Central Missouri and the Little Rock Conferences were placed in the Saint Louis Area. The Lexington Conference was placed in the Indianapolis Area.[4] All these areas were integrated.

First Negro Woman Licensed to Preach

For many quadrennia, the General Conferences had been flooded with petitions urging that women be granted the privilege of receiving local license. The 1920 Episcopal Address expressed the opinion of the church fathers in this statement:

> These boards and institutions that directly touch youth in the years when it is making its life decision ought to have coordinated, systematized plans, not for an occasional campaign of recruiting and training but for a continuous unwearying regard for gathering *men and women for the ministry and other forms of special Christian endeavor.*[5]

On May 20, 1920, the General Conference authorized that local license could be granted to women in the Methodist Episcopal Church.

The Upper Mississippi Conference claims the honor of being the first Negro Conference to grant local preacher's license to a woman. On June 12, 1920, the Greenwood District granted local preacher's license to Mrs. Mary E. Jones of Indianola, Mississippi.[6] She was recommended by the Indianola Quarterly Conference. The district superintendent was J. W. Golden. The Reverend W. C. Conwell was pastor in charge.

The First Black General Superintendent Presides Over His First Annual Conference

On Wednesday, November 11, 1920, all eyes in Methodism were turned toward Alexandria City, Alabama. On that day, this small Alabama town was to make history. It was to entertain the Central Alabama Annual Conference of the Methodist Episcopal Church. It would be different— the presiding bishop would be a black man.

At 8:30 A.M., Bishop Robert Elijah Jones called the Central Alabama Conference to order in the Haven Memorial Church. He used a gavel that had historic significance. It was first used in the General Conference of 1892 in Omaha, Nebraska. It had also been used in the General

Conference of the Methodist Episcopal Church South. Forty-four bishops had used it previously.[7]

The conference opened by singing one of Wesley's Hymns: "And Are We Yet Alive." This hymn had been used in the opening of Methodist Conferences for a century and a half throughout the world.

The conference organized with the election of J. B. F. Shaw, president of Central Alabama Institute, as its secretary. S. C. Walker was elected statistician and A. S. Williams was elected treasurer.

On November 14, 1920, Bishop R. E. Jones ordained John H. Duffie as a deacon in the church. He ordained the following men as elders: Albert R. Neal, Isaac B. Points, Sydney B. Thornton and Peter V. Woffard.[8] These men have the honor of being the first black preachers to be ordained by a black general superintendent.

Bishop Jones presented the following short range and long range objectives to the conference:

(1) Increased loyalty to God and the Church.
(2) Rekindling of the evangelistic fires in the Church.
(3) Stewardship and tithing.
(4) Education and Life Service.
(5) Recruitment for full-time Christian work.
(6) The total Centenary Program.

The annual conference approved these objectives. These objectives developed into his philosophy of administration.

In every annual conference over which he presided thereafter, he emphasized winning souls to Christ and paying World Service in full. He believed that World Service was the heartbeat of Methodism.

His emphasis upon World Service produced increased giving for World Service in all the conferences over which he presided. During his first quadrennium, the New Orleans Area raised $462,190 for World Service.[9] This area raised only $80,041 for the previous quadrennium.

The Establishment of Gulfside Assembly

Perhaps the most outstanding achievement of Bishop Jones during his first quadrennium was the establishment of Gulfside Assembly. It was a dream fulfilled.

Very early after his election to the episcopacy, he was invited to the Lakeside Assembly in Ohio as a guest speaker. While there, he was motivated to establish a similar institution for his people on the Gulf of Mexico.

Immediately on his return to New Orleans, he began a search for a favorable location. He found a place on the Gulf of Mexico at Waveland, Mississippi. It was purchased in fee simple title. In addition, he secured a lease of shoreline of over a mile. It was only forty-eight miles from New Orleans. Several trains stopped at Waveland daily.

Included on the property leased was a hotel, the old historic Jackson house. It was erected by the nephew of Andrew Jackson. This building served as the only housing facility until others could be erected.

On January 28, 1924, the Gulfside Assembly was incorporated in the state of Mississippi. The following men were the incorporators: Robert E. Jones, E. M. Jones, William Robinson, M. W. Dogan, M. S. Davage, William Jones, T. F. Robinson, L. H. King, R. N. Brooks, S. W. Brown, M. T. J. Howard, J. W. Golden, J. F. Farmer, Sr., P. H. Rembert, C. S. Briggs, and M. R. Walker.

The Gulfside Assembly has served as a Chautauqua for black people in the South. It has served as a center of continuing education for ministers and laymen. A "Poor boy" school was established in the beginning. This school enabled deprived functional illiterates to develop salable skills. Several have gone from this school and prepared themselves for the Christian ministry.

It has served as a meeting place for ecumenical and interracial groups. Several civic groups have used the facilities here. In fact, it has been a "Mecca" for black people for a half century.

85

More Black Conferences Under Black Leadership

In 1924, the General Conference placed more black conferences under black leadership. The Covington Area was created. To this area, Bishop M. W. Clair, Sr., was assigned. In addition to the supervision of the Liberia Conference, the following black conferences were placed in the Covington Area: Central Missouri, Lincoln, Lexington and Little Rock. By 1924, ten conferences were supervised by black bishops.

The Third Black General Superintendent

In 1912, the General Conference established a mandatory age of retirement for bishops. They were required to retire at the age nearest their seventy-third birthday.

In 1936, Bishop M. W. Clair, Sr., reached the age of mandatory retirement. He was retired at the 1936 General Conference. On May 14, 1936, Alexander Preston Shaw from the Upper Mississippi Conference was elected general superintendent.[10] He was the third Negro to be elected. He was not a member of the 1936 General Conference.

For residential and presidential supervision, Bishop A. P. Shaw was assigned to the New Orleans Area. Bishop Jones was assigned to the Covington Area for the quadrennium of 1936–40 as Bishop Clair's successor.

The Plan of Union and the Negro

The Plan of Union among the Methodist Episcopal Church, the Methodist Protestant Church and the Methodist Episcopal Church South was developed over a period of a century. The first seven decades were described by Bishop J. M. Moore as an "era of conflict and distrust." The last three decades showed progress in real negotiation.

It soon became evident that some burning issues had to

be resolved before merger could be consummated. The first was conflicting political philosophies.

The Church North adhered strictly to the philosophy of Federalism and Centralization as advocated by Alexander Hamilton.[11] He was a staunch supporter of a strong national government. He was opposed to placing too much power in the hands of the people. He argued that unless the constitution forbade it, all was allowed. Contrariwise, the Church South adhered to the political philosophy of regionalism as advocated by Thomas Jefferson. Jefferson recognized the nation to be composed of agrarian and self-governing states. The ultimate authority lay in the consent of the governed. He argued that the powers of Federal government was limited to that which was only expressed in the Constitution.

The powers of the General Conference had to be defined to the satisfaction of both sections of the country. The Church North viewed the General Conference as the sole authority. It was the legislative and the judicial authority. The Church South gave bishops unlimited authority. In addition, the acts of the General Conference could be ratified by vote of annual conferences.

The Negro problem could not be shunted. It had to be faced. There were many viewpoints expressed. Some advocated the establishment of a central conference in the United States for Negroes. Others recommended that the Negroes be encouraged to unite with other black Methodist denominations and form a United Black Methodist Church. Others had political fears. It was believed that the Negroes would vote always on the side of the Northern church. The Southern branch would be at a disadvantage politically.

A commission was established to find a solution to these and other problems involved in union. Representatives from all three branches of Methodism were included. The three Negro members of the commission were: Bishop R. E. Jones, Dr. I. Garland Penn and Dr. W. J. King.

After many years of study, the commission recommended that the Plan of Union must include the following:

(1) The name of the Church would be the Methodist Church.

(2) The Articles of Religion were to be those historically held by all three denominations.

(3) Episcopacy would be the form of government. The Methodist Protestant Church would elect two General Superintendents.

(4) The General Conference would have legislative powers over all connectional matters.

(5) There would be five regional jurisdictions in the United States. In addition, there would be a Central Jurisdiction to include all Negro Conferences.

(6) Equal representation between clergy and laymen in the General and Jurisdictional Conferences.

(7) There would be a Judicial Council. It would have the final authority in interpreting the law. The members of this council would be elected by the General Conference.[12]

The Ratification of the Plan of Union

In order that union could be consummated, it was necessary for all three General Conferences of participating denominations to vote approval. It was also necessary for the two-thirds majority of the total number of votes cast in annual conferences of each denomination to approve the Plan of Union.

The Methodist Protestant Church was the first denomination to ratify the Plan of Union. Its General Conference approved it by 142 for and 39 against.[13] Twenty of the 25 annual conferences voted in the affirmative, which was more than two-thirds majority for adoption.

The Methodist Episcopal Church was the next to take action. On May 14, 1936, its General Conference approved the Plan of Union by 470 for to 83 against. Although it was approved overwhelmingly by the General Conference, thirty-six Negro delegates voted against the plan and eleven abstained. After the General Conference approved the plan, it was sent down to the annual conferences for action. The annual conferences approved the plan by 17,239 in favor and 1,832 against the plan.

The Negro conferences voted by orders. The total votes by clergy for the plan were 551; 681 voted against the plan. The lay voted 249 for the plan and 408 against the plan. Thirteen conferences failed to ratify the Plan of Union.[14] Four conferences ratified the plan. Two conferences did not vote on the plan inasmuch as its adoption was *fait accompli*.

The majority of black leaders did not approve of the plan. They used every effort possible to abort the birth of the Central Jurisdiction. They used the printer's ink unsparingly to express their views.

Leaders voiced their opposition at the 1936 General Conference. The late Bishop R. N. Brooks said: "If you are going to throw us overboard, please untie our hands." The late David D. Jones, president of Bennett College, declared, "You may adopt this plan, we are powerless to prevent it. All we can do is to appeal to time." The veteran Negro educator, Matthew S. Davage, stated: "We want to be in a church which embraces all mankind and is big enough for God." Bishop Willis J. King described it as a "symbol of racial exclusiveness."

Among the many reasons enumerated for rejecting the Plan of Union, the following are cited:

(1) The plan wrote segregation into the constitution of the church.
(2) The plan discriminated against the Negroes. Discrimination is a denial of the dignity of man, subverts the union to which all Christians have in Christ, and stultifies the mission of the church.
(3) The Blacks opposed because it put union above brotherhood. Blacks believe in ecumenicity but they refused to be "ecumaniacs."
(4) The Central Jurisdiction was a segregated structural arrangement. All other jurisdictions were regional and included all Methodist in the regions.

The last denomination to vote on the plan was the Methodist Episcopal Church South. Due to the fact that its General Conference did not meet until 1938, it voted in reverse order. The annual conferences voted first. In 1937, the annual conferences of the Church South ratified the plan by 7,652 for and 1,247 against. Only one conference failed to ratify it.[15]

In 1938, the General Conference of this church approved the plan. It voted 434 in favor to 26 against.

In 1939, the Uniting Conference convened in Kansas City, Missouri. On May 10, 1939, the Methodist Church became a reality. At 8:59 P.M., the presiding officer declared: "The Declaration of Union has been adopted. The Methodist Church now is."

The Negro became the "sacrificial lamb" on the altar in order that union could be consummated. It was indeed an exorbitant price to pay for church union.

CHAPTER VII

The Central Jurisdiction—The Price for Union, 1940–1974

Chapter VI described the creation of the Central Jurisdiction. This chapter proposes to indicate the reluctant acceptance of the will of the majority by the Negroes in the church. In the message of the College of Bishops of the First Central Jurisdictional Conference, Bishop Robert E. Jones, the senior bishop of the jurisdiction, expressed the reluctance in these words:

> After the Negro had registered his opinion and had been outvoted by a majority in the three churches, he logically and loyally submitted to the outcome.[1]

But the people of the Central Jurisdiction were determined that this "symbol of racial exclusiveness" would be short-lived.

The leaders of the jurisdiction accepted the Central Jurisdiction as a temporary expedient. In 1944, Bishop A. P. Shaw expressed it in these words:

> We are not in harmony with any Methodists or others who think such a plan necessary in a truly Christian brotherhood. We consider it expedient only on account of the Christian childhood of some American Methodists who

91

need a little coddling until they can grow into full grown manhood and womanhood in Christ Jesus. We are hopeful that in the very near future our Methodism may become sufficiently Christian in character and maturity to find a more excellent way.[2]

While black Methodists waited patiently for some churchmen to reach maturity in Christian character, it became the corporate resolve to "strengthen what remains."

Strenuous efforts were made to enrich their worship experiences, upgrade the church facilities, and recruit and train more lay and ministerial leaders.

Emphases were placed upon evangelism, Christian education, missions, and stewardship in every local church. Prodigious efforts were made to organize a board of lay activities and a woman's society of Christian service in each church.

During this first quadrennium, high priority was placed upon Christian education. Full-time executive secretaries of Christian education were employed.

Help From the General Church

In efforts to strengthen the churches in the Central Jurisdiction, the General Conference lent a helping hand. In 1948, the General Conference broadened the recipients of Crusade Scholarships to include ethnic minorities within the United States. It was still limited to those preparing for full-time Christian work. In 1968, the General Conference gave another dimension to the Crusade Scholarship program. It was thereafter to include persons who were preparing to "work in the church and society." Since 1948, 252 blacks have been recipients of Crusade Scholarships.

The general boards and agencies assisted the conferences in their efforts to improve facilities, upgrading of skills, and training of lay and ministerial leadership. The Board of Education assisted the black colleges in helping them to become fully accredited by the regional accrediting agencies. It employed Dr. M. S. Davage and assigned to him the following tasks: (1) raising funds within the church for the Negro colleges; (2) promoting Race Relations Day. He was very successful in these tasks. In 1940, the Methodist contributed $27,363 on Race Relations Day. In 1952, the church had increased its annual giving to Negro colleges to $239,000.[3] The Division of Local Churches of the Board of Education assisted the conferences by providing leadership training opportunities for its church leaders.

The General Board of Missions likewise contributed to the strengthening of the local churches. It provided financial assistance and served also in a consultative role.

It provided salary supplement for many pastors of the Central Jurisdiction. The Church Extension Department assisted in renovation and erecting of churches and parsonages. Loans were granted at low interest rates. Some churches were granted donations. It also provided architectural assistance for the mission churches. In some cases, church builders were provided to erect churches and parsonages.

The Crusade for Christ and the Negro

In 1944, the General Conference adopted as its quadrennial program: "The Crusade For Christ." It was Methodism's way of responding to the many needs of people resulting from the war.

In responding to the needs, Black Conferences evidenced their stewardship responsibility. The apportionment to the Central Jurisdiction was $796,300. The Jurisdiction raised $770,330.37.[4]

The first episcopal area of Methodism to pay its quota in full was the New Orleans area. Its quota was $223.375. The area paid $227,249.50 by April 26, 1945. Six other conferences paid their full quotas: Atlanta, Central Alabama, Delaware, Florida, North Carolina, and South Carolina.

The Slow Death of the Central Jurisdiction

The Central Jurisdiction was designed by some to be a temporary expedient. Others planned to institutionalize it and continue it as a permanent structural arrangement. It died a slow death. Before it died, it passed through three stages. The first period may be described as the period of proclamation and study. The second period was voluntary integration. The last stage was mandatory integration.

The Period of Proclamation and Study, 1944–1956

For twelve years, the General Conference passed resolutions and appointed study committees. In 1944, the General Conference declared: "We look to the ultimate elimination of racial discrimination in the Methodist Church." It also appointed its first study committee. Its function was to "consider afresh the relations of all races included in the membership of the Methodist Church and to report back to the 1948 General Conference."

The 1948 General Conference delegates listened in rapt attention to the presentation of the report. It then expressed appreciation for the report and referred it to the boards and agencies "for systematic use in their activities and publication." It authorized another study on social issues.

The black delegates left the Boston General Conference disappointed indeed. They decided to seek for themselves a viable solution to the race problem in the church. The 1948 Central Jurisdictional Conference authorized a study commission within the jurisdiction. Its purpose was "to study the Central Jurisdiction with a view to determine its advantages and its disadvantages, its relationship to other jurisdictions." It was authorized to report to the 1952 Jurisdictional Conference. This jurisdictional conference also requested that President Truman issue an executive order abolishing segregation in the Armed Forces.

On August 28, 1951, Bishop Robert N. Brooks delivered a masterful address on "Fishing in Troubled Waters." He described segregation and discrimination as Methodism's twin evils. Said he:

> It is the twin evils of discrimination and segregation that the Church has failed so lamentably. It has by its practices, sanctified the racial prejudice which is rampart in the world today . . . but it cannot say a convincing word to society unless and until its eliminates these cancerous evils from its own Christian community.[5]

In the 1952 Episcopal Address, Bishop Paul Kern declared:

> To discriminate against a person solely upon the basis of his race is both unfair and unChristian. Every child of God is entitled to that place in society which he has won by his industry, his integrity and his character.[6]

These classic words were so provocative that both the 1956 and the 1960 Episcopal Addresses referred to them.

The only significant action regarding the abolition of the Central Jurisdiction by this 1952 General Conference was to allow local churches to transfer from one jurisdiction to another jurisdiction. It was the beginning of the effort to abolish the Central Jurisdiction by a method of attrition.

Before the 1956 General Conference convened in Minneapolis, Minnesota, the "walls of segregation" had been cracked. The social iceberg had begun to thaw very slowly.

In 1950, President Harry Truman issued an executive order to end segregation in the Armed Services. In addition, the Supreme Court had rendered one of its most significant decisions affecting Negroes in sixty years. On May 17, 1954, it declared that "separate educational facilities are inherently unequal." On May 31, 1955, this court issued a mandate that schools must be desegregated "with all deliberate speed."

With the "walls of segregation" being cracked, some delegates went to the 1956 General Conference determined to move out of the stage of pronouncement into action.

THE PERIOD OF VOLUNTARY INTEGRATION, 1956–1966

The second stage was the gradual abolition of the Central Jurisdiction. It was based upon the principle of voluntarism. Although the church had begun to move in the right direction, it was moving at a snail-like pace.

The 1956 General Conference was the beginning of this period of voluntary integration. On May 1, 1956, this conference adopted the following statement on race:

> There must be no place in the Methodist Church for racial discrimination or enforced segregation, recognizing that we have not attained this goal, yet rejoicing in the progress made, we recommend that discrimination or segregation by any method or practice whether in conference structure or otherwise be abolished with reasonable speed.[7]

It is significant to note that the General Conference used the phrase, "with reasonable speed." The Supreme Court had used, earlier, the phrase, "with deliberate speed."

On May 2, 1956, the Minneapolis General Conference approved an instrument to facilitate the abolition of the Central Jurisdiction. Amendment IX was approved. It permitted the transfer of churches to other annual conferences providing it had prior approval by the quarterly conference and both annual conferences involved.

This constitutional amendment was approved by the annual conferences. The black conferences voted overwhelmingly in favor of the amendment. Eight black conferences voted unanimously, the nine other conferences voted by two-thirds majority. Only seventy-one negative votes were cast in the Central Jurisdiction.

When the 1960 General Conference convened, it was time to take stock of the effectiveness of the instrument. Those in favor of the instrument debated that time was too short to evaluate its effectiveness. Others argued that it was a too slow process. Furthermore, it was a piecemeal approach. It was abolishing the Central Jurisdiction by attrition. The black leaders agreed that it was too slow.

Efforts were made to establish a "target date" for the elimination of the Central Jurisdiction. The Report of the Commission on Interjurisdictional Relations recommended that there would be "no basic change in the regional juris-dictional system."

One strong advocate of establishing a target date was Harold Case, Boston University. He offered the following amendment to the report:

> . . . shall have in part as their express goal the abolition of the Central Jurisdiction by due constitutional process by 1968.[8]

Black delegates approved of this amendment. In support of the amendment, Charles F. Golden, Lexington Conference, said:

> Certainly, there will be a price to be paid for progress made, but this amendment will give us opportunity to lift the level of performance in the conferences of the Central Jurisdiction, particularly in the area of leadership training, salaries, pension rates and other differences that increase the gap between conferences of the Central Jurisdiction and over-lapping geographic jurisdictions.[9]

The Case Amendment lost. The report was adopted as printed.

The black delegates left this conference smarting under defeat but determined to find a viable solution. More than ever, they were ready to press their claim.

The 1960 Central Jurisdictional Conference lost no time in its effort to press its claim. It approved of a Committee of Five. Its task was threefold: (1) prepare a report indicating in crystal clear language what the Negroes expected of the church (there was an audibility gap between the blacks in the Methodist Church and their white brethren); (2) analyze the recommendation of the Commission on Interjurisdictional Relations and make its recommendations to the conferences of the Central Jurisdiction; and (3) Develop a plan of action for the Central Jurisdiction and devise strategies for implementing the Plan of Action.

On July 12, 1960, the College of Bishops appointed the following persons to constitute the Committee of Five:

James S. Thomas	Atlantic Coast Area
Richard Erwin	Baltimore Area
John H. Graham	Nashville-Birmingham Area
W. Astor Kirk	New Orleans Area
John J. Hicks	Saint Louis Area

In order to prepare a report for the church, the committee proposed a study conference.

A Study Conference was convened in Cincinnati, Ohio, March 26–28, 1961. Participants in this conference were all bishops, district superintendents, pastors, women, laymen, youth, executive secretaries of Christian education, college presidents, and representatives of the general boards and agencies of the church.

For many hours, these leaders worked assidiously to prepare a document which would indicate their expectations of the Church. From this study conference came the document entitled: "Central Jurisdiction Speaks." The following principles were articulated:

(1) The fundamental objective in the dissolution of the Central Jurisdiction must be *de facto* inclusiveness in the Methodist Church.

(2) The minimum requirement of *de facto* inclusiveness

98

is the absence on all levels of church life of patterns and policies based on race or color.

(3) Each step taken to dissolve the Central Jurisdiction must be an integral part of an overall plan or program to abolish all forms of racial segregation and discrimination from the Methodist Church.[10]

In addition to the cardinal principles articulated, the Study Conference recommended the following basic procedures: (1) a Plan should be completed to realign all annual conferences presented to the 1964 Jurisdictional Conference for action; (2) standards or criteria should be set to guide local churches and annual conferences with respect to all matters of transfer under Amendment IX; and (3) each annual conference should designate an agency or board to examine resolutions and make recommendation to the annual conference.

Another task of the committee was to examine the recommendations from the Commission on Interjurisdictional Relations. On April 29, 1961, this commission released report number 1.

The commission recommended that the conferences of the Baltimore Area would be transferred to the Northeastern Jurisdiction. The Saint Louis Area would be transferred to the North Central Jurisdiction. The New Orleans Area would be transferred into the South Central Jurisdiction. The Atlantic Coast Area and the Nashville-Birmingham Area would be transferred into the Southeastern Jurisdiction.

The Committee of Five viewed the report as being reprehensible. It violated the principles that the Cincinnati Study Committee had approved. The plan of the commission would have institutionalized a system of racially segregated annual conferences in regional jurisdictions. The plan failed further to deal with the crucial problems of racial segregation and discrimination in the government, programs and institutions of the church.

When the 1964 General Conference convened in Pittsburgh, Pennsylvania, the Central Jurisdiction was still a segregated structural arrangement in the Church. Amendment IX had only been used by a few churches.

Pressure for the elimination of the Central Jurisdiction was mounting. In addition, this conference was the first to be picketed by demonstrators seeking redress from the social injustices rampant in American Society.

The Episcopal Address set the stage for action. Bishop Gerald Kennedy expressed the sentiments and judgment of the Fathers of the Church in these words:

> We believe that this General Conference should insist upon the removal from its structure of any mark of racial segregation and do it without wasting time . . . God Almighty is moving toward a world of interracial brotherhood so speedily and irresitably that to hesitate is to fight against God and be crushed.[11]

The 1964 General Conference took several significant actions regarding segregation in the Church. It decreed that all local churches must be opened to all persons without regard to race, color, national origin or economic condition. By this action it was only placing in the Discipline of the Methodist Church a mandate that was put in the Discipline of the Methodist Episcopal Church in 1884.

Three other important actions were taken. The conference adopted a detailed plan of action, pursuant to which the Central Jurisdiction would realign its conferences so that each annual conference and episcopal area would be located in only one regional jurisdiction. The Committee of Five had so recommended.

To facilitate transfers and mergers, the General Conference approved of a temporary general aid fund. This fund was to be used in the upgrading of the minimum salaries and pension benefits for the Central Jurisdiction's ministers.

Another timely action was the creation of a Commission on Interjurisdictional Relations. Its task was to facilitate the dissolution of the Central Jurisdiction and the integration of the conferences. This was the first action taken regarding *de facto* inclusiveness.

Advisory councils were approved. They were to be organized in each jurisdiction. These councils were designed to engage the regional jurisdictions in creative dialogue with the Central Jurisdiction. This proved to be very fruitful indeed. For the first time people were able to sit together and seek a viable solution.

The black delegates left this General Conference content but not satisfied. They were determined to keep their pledge to realign the conferences.

The 1964 Central Jurisdictional Conference convened in Daytona Beach, Florida. At this conference the Committee of Five made its report to the conference under the caption of "Bridges to Racial Equality in the Church."[12]

The committee's report included the following recommendations:

(1) That the Central Jurisdiction reaffirm its commitment to the fundamental goal of a society and fellowship of Methodist Christians completely uncircumscribed at all levels of church life by distinctions based on race or color.

(2) That the Central Jurisdictional Conference would unequivocally affirm its opposition to segregated annual conferences in regional jurisdictions.

(3) That all the conferences and areas be realigned so that they would be located in only one geographic jurisdiction.

The Jurisdictional Conference adopted this report overwhelmingly. There were only a few minor amendments included.

The Committee on the Episcopacy presented its report to the conference. It recommended the realignment of conferences and areas in keeping with the report of the Committee of Five. The areas were reconstituted and renamed, and the

101

bishops were assigned to supervise conferences in only one regional jurisdiction.

The Central Jurisdictional Conference convened earlier than other jurisdictional conferences in order that they could take whatever action they desired. The North Central Jurisdictional Conference merged the Lexington Conferences with its overlapping conferences in 1964. This Conference assigned Bishop James S. Thomas to the Iowa Area. At the close of this conference, there was no racial conference structures in its boundary.

The Northeastern Jurisdiction continued the Washington and Delaware Conferences for one year. These conferences were placed in the Washington Area. The New Jersey Area was created. The conference assigned Bishop Prince A. Taylor to that area. After 1965, there were no racial conferences structures in the Northeastern Jurisdiction.

In 1966, the Central West Conference merged with the Missouri West and Missouri East Conference. Churches and ministers had been previously transferred to the Western Jurisdiction under Amendment IX.

The remnant Central Jurisdiction remained as an emaciated segregated structure in the Constitution of the Church. There were still twelve racial conferences constituting the Central Jurisdiction.

MANDATORY INTEGRATION, THE PERIOD OF 1966–1974

The 1966 General Conference was an adjourned session of the 1964 General Conference. Its chief business was to vote on the Plan of Union with the Evangelical United Brethren Church.

Efforts were made by the leaders of the Central Jurisdiction to attach a rider to the Plan of Union. They felt that the Methodist Church should set its house in order before merging with another denomination. In these words, Major Jones, Tennessee-Kentucky Conference, expressed it:

> It would be a greater sin to carry these structures over into union—for us not to solve this problem by some definite time for elimination of the Central Jurisdiction.[13]

In addition, efforts were made to amend the report of the Commission of Interjurisdictional Relations. A sincere effort was made by Joseph E. Lowery to amend the report in these words:

> It is determined that all necessary steps will be taken to eliminate any structural organization in the Methodist Church based on race at the earliest possible date; and not later than three months prior to the 1972 General Conference.[14]

The amendment did not prevail.

The General Conference adopted the Plan of Union. With its adoption, the church entered the third stage of the abolition of the Central Jurisdiction. The Plan of Union did not include the Central Jurisdiction in its Constitution after its final adoption in 1968.

Many Negro leaders refused to vote for the Plan of Union. In addition, they conducted a "pray-in" to illustrate their disapproval of the plan. It did remove the Central Jurisdiction from a segregated structural arrangement in the constitution, but it did not provide for integrated conferences.

The year 1967 brought mixed emotions to the black people in the Central Jurisdiction. In August, the last Central Jurisdictional Conference was held. In addition to electing the last bishop by the Central Jurisdiction, emphasis was upon moving the segregated conferences in the South Central and Southeastern Jurisdictions into integrated conferences.

With the Central Jurisdiction being abolished, it was expected that the *Central Christian Advocate* would be abolished very soon. What would be the voice of the black people now?

In that year, a group of interested black churchmen organized the Black Methodists for Church Renewal. This body was created to communicate the new self image and mood of the black community to the church. It stressed church renewal. Renewal must come through the redistribution of power.

The body sought also to sensitize the church to the many needs of black people. It served as a gadfly during the transitional period of the church.

Black Methodist for Church Renewal emphasized self-determination from its inception. It defined self-determination as the process of oppressed ethnic groups defining themselves and their world in terms of their real needs and aspirations.

This organization stressed black empowerment within the church. It developed community action programs and programs of economic development as a means of empowering people.

By the end of 1967, all conferences had been transferred into regional jurisdictions with the exception of three. The Georgia, South Carolina, and the Tennessee Conferences remained as the remnant of Central Jurisdiction.

When the 1968 General Conference convened in Dallas, these three conferences were transferred into the Southeastern Jurisdiction by mandatory action. With this action, the Central Jurisdiction as a segregated structural arrangement in the constitution of the Church had been abolished. There were still ten segregated conferences.

The Dallas Conference created the Commission of Religion and Race. Its primary responsibility was "to facilitate mergers of conferences, provide counsel to churches seeking to become a truly inclusive fellowship." In addition, it was to have administration of the Temporary General Aid Fund. It was to also see that minority groups were adequately represented on Boards and Agencies of the Church.

Still at a snail-like pace, racially structured conferences continued to merge with regional annual conferences. In 1968, black churches in Tennessee and Kentucky were transferred into the regional conferences. In 1969, the two Florida conferences were merged.

The special session of the General Conference in 1970 took two significant actions affecting the black constituency. It reordered priorities in support of the principal of determination of minority groups. Another action was the approval of a single pension rate in merged conferences. This action removed another barrier in the merging of conferences.

This was the third General Conference in Methodism that adjourned early due to the lack of the quorum. Both the 1816 and 1860 General Conferences also did so. Many petitions were left on the calendar due to the adjournment.

In 1970 and 1971, four other black conferences were merged with regional conferences. In 1970, the Louisiana, Texas, and West Conferences merged with regional conferences. In 1971, the Georgia Conference merged with the North and South Georgia Conferences.

When the 1972 General Conference convened in Atlanta, Georgia, there were still five black conferences. Four—Central Alabama, Mississippi, Upper Mississippi, South Carolina— were in the Southeastern Jurisdiction. The Southwest Conference was in the South Central Jurisdiction.

On April 27, 1972, the General Conference issued a mandate to these conferences in these words:

> The General Conference hereby directs the remaining racially structured annual conferences and the eight annual conferences with which overlap to take all steps necessary to consummate mergers at the earliest possible date, the initial action to be taken in their sessions of 1972 and to be concluded not later than their regular session of 1973, and in any event not later than July 1, 1973.[15]

It took contingency action as well. It authorized a board of arbitration to be composed of the president of the five colleges of bishops.

In June, 1972, the conferences in South Carolina were merged. By the mandatory deadline, all conferences had merged.

By 1974, segregated institutional structures had been eliminated on the associative level. The acid test of *de facto* inclusiveness is on the local church level. Chapter IX will discuss it.

FUTILE EFFORTS TO KEEP THE CENTRAL JURISDICTION ALIVE

In 1966, the General Conference set a date for the termination of the Central Jurisdiction as a segregated structure. Upon the adoption of the Plan of Union with the Evangelical United Brethren Church, there was no provision made for the Central Jurisdiction. Hence, the Central Jurisdiction had only two years to live.

When the death of the Central Jurisdiction became imminent, a few blacks and whites began immediately to employ the "respirator of political maneuverings," to prolong the life of this already emaciated institutional structure.

It is strange indeed, but some of these individuals had spoken so passionately in earlier general conferences in favor of eliminating the Central Jurisdiction immediately; others had participated in the "kneel-in" at the 1966 General Conference.

On March 9, 1967, the Central Jurisdictional Advisory Council voted by a two-thirds majority in support of the General Conference's recommendation. From every episcopal area of the jurisdiction, individuals supported the resolution. Despite this fact, strenuous efforts were made to prevent annual conferences from approving the resolution by the necessary two-thirds majority.

The Georgia Conference was the first conference to defeat the resolution. After this conference defeated the resolution, other conferences were urged to do likewise. The opponents of the resolution implied that one conference had veto power. Unless all the conferences voted favorably, it would not prevail. They did not convince but three conferences.

Efforts were still exerted to prolong the life of the Central

Jurisdiction. It was referred to the Judicial Council for a decision. The Judicial Council issued its decision on February 5, 1968. It declared that all constitutional requirements had been met.[16]

All efforts to save the Central Jurisdiction failed. On April 23, 1968, at approximately 9:30 A.M., Bishop Reuben Mueller and Bishop Lloyd C. Wicke joined hands over the Plan of Union and said:

Lord of the Church, we are united in thee; in Thy Church and now in the United Methodist Church.

By this declaration, the Central Jurisdiction was pronounced dead.

CHAPTER VIII

Special Honors and Distinguished Leadership Roles of Black Methodists in the Church and Society

This chapter will enumerate a limited number of black leaders in the church and society. By leadership is meant an ascribed role over a relatively long period of time. Leadership is never assumed but always ascribed.

A few black Methodists have been awarded special honors. Others will be included because of their role ascription in the Church and Society.

Special Honor Awards

Citation must be given to Emma P. Hill. After the General Conference of 1956 voted full clergy rights to women, she was the first black woman to be admitted into annual conference on trial. The Washington Conference admitted her on trial on May 24, 1956. She was appointed to the Saint Luke Church on the Washington District.

Four black Methodists have been honored by their election to the Judicial Council of the Church. On May 7, 1948, Attorney J. Ernest Wilkins was the first black to be elected. Again, he was elected for the second term on May 7, 1956. He was the first black to serve as president of the Judicial

Council. He served with distinction until his untimely death on January 19, 1959. He was a member of the Saint Marks Church, Chicago, Illinois.

The second black layman to be elected to the Judicial Council was Attorney Theodore M. Berry. He was elected on May 4, 1960. He served for two terms. He was a member of the Mount Zion Church in Cincinnati, Ohio.

On May 1, 1968, the first black clergyman was elected. The Reverend Charles Buchanan Copher of the North Georgia Conference was elected. He is now serving his third term.

The first black laywoman to be elected was Mrs. Florence Little Edwards. She was elected on April 26, 1972. She is a member of the Brooks Memorial Church, Jamaica, New York.

At least six black ministers have made a career by serving in the Armed Forces as chaplains. The Reverend Elmer P. Gibson, Delaware Conference, served in the regular Army from 1941 to 1962. He won the Bronze Star. He retired as lieutenant colonel. The Reverend Ernest L. Harrison, Upper Mississippi Conference, served with distinction from 1945 to 1965. He retired as a major in the Army Reserve. The Reverend George W. Williams, South Carolina Conference, served from 1942 to 1967 in the regular Army. He was awarded the Decorated Bronze Star and the Silver Star. He retired as lieutenant colonel. The Reverend John W. Handy, Jr., Delaware Conference, served as chaplain from 1943 to 1961. He too was awarded the Decorated Bronze Star medal and four Battle Stars. He retired as colonel. He is the first black chaplain in the United Methodist Church to hold the rank of colonel. The Reverend Norman G. Long, Lexington Conference, served as chaplain from 1937 to 1968. He retired as lieutenant colonel on February 28, 1968. The Reverend Pliny W. Jenkins, North Carolina Conference, served for twenty years. He retired as a lieutenant colonel on July 31, 1961.

Two lay persons have been elected as presidents of boards or divisions. In 1972, the General Council on Ministry elected Dr. John T. King, president of Huston-Tillotson College, as its first president. In 1976, the Woman's Division of Christian Service of the Board of Global Ministries elected Mrs. Mai Gray of Missouri as its first black president.

Black Veterans in General Conference

It is assumed that a person elected to ten or more General Conferences merits the honor of being called a veteran. When a person is elected to the General Conference for the first time, it is an accident. When he or she is elected to ten or more general conferences, it is a significant achievement.

There are five black persons who have achieved this honor. They are Reverend E. M. Jones, Mr. Herbert S. Wilson, Dr. Matthew S. Davage, the Reverend Matthew Dogan, and Mr. Irwin Garland Penn.

The Reverend Edward M. Jones was elected by his peers to thirteen General Conferences. In 1896, he was elected for the first time. He was elected as a delegate to every successive General Conference and Uniting Conference until 1944. After he retired, the Central Alabama Conference elected him to lead its delegation in 1943.

He was a "crescive leader" in his conference. He was respected by his peers. He was affectionately called "Uncle Emmer" by his peers in later life. He died in 1944.

The second black to be so honored in rank order was Herbert S. Wilson. He was a layman. He was a merchant in Upper Hill, Maryland. He was a member of the Saint Andrew Methodist Church. He was elected to twelve General Conferences and the Uniting Conference in 1939.

The other three veterans tied for third place. The Reverend Matthew Dogan, Dr. M. S. Davage, and Mr. I. Garland Penn served in ten General Conferences.

The Reverend Matthew Dogan was first elected by the Texas Conference in 1904. He was elected every time by the

110

ministerial delegates of the Texas Conference on the first ballot. He was the president of Wiley College for forty years. He has the longest tenure as a president of any in the black institutions. He died June 17, 1947.

Three conferences—Louisiana, Upper Mississippi, and West Texas—honored Dr. M. S. Davage by electing him as a lay delegate to the General Conference. He was first elected by the Louisiana Conference in 1908. He died September 20, 1976.

Another layman to merit the role of a veteran was Mr. Irvin Garland Penn. He was first elected by the Washington Conference in 1892. He was a member of Asbury Methodist Church, Washington, D. C. He served as secretary of the Board of Education from 1912 until his death on July 22, 1930.

Black Pastors with Long Tenure in the Same Parish

Prior to 1900, the time limit of a pastor in the same parish was five years. The 1900 General Conference removed the time limit.

Since the time limit was removed, there have been twenty-two men at least who have served twenty years or more in the same parish. The following men are cited:

1. The Reverend F. A. Cullen has the longest pastorate in the same church. He served the Salem Church, New York for thirty-four years. He served here from 1908 to 1942. He retired in 1942. He died May 25, 1946.
2. On John's Island, South Carolina, Giles C. Brown served for thirty-two years. He retired in 1967.
3. On the Dover District of the Delaware Conference, J. O. Lockman served Lincoln City also for thirty-two years (1929–1961). He died November 6, 1961.
4. The Tindley Temple Church, Philadelphia, Pennsylvania, was served by the Reverend Charles A. Tindley for thirty-one years. He died July 26, 1933.
5. The Union Memorial Church, Saint Louis, Missouri,

111

was served by B. F. Abbott for thirty-one years also. After this long tenure, he was placed on the Saint Louis District. He died on June 6, 1944.

6. The Reverend Eleazer Rakestraw was appointed to the Wesley Church for thirty years. He died January 3, 1967.

7. The Reverend Henry H. Nichols has the longest tenure of any black Pastor today. He has served the Jane United Methodist Church, Philadelphia, Pennsylvania, since 1946.

8. The next in time order is the Reverend Ira Benjamin Loud. He has served the Saint Paul United Methodist Church in Dallas, Texas, since 1948.

9. The Reverend Hamilton T. Boswell served the Jones Memorial United Methodist Church, San Francisco, California for twenty-nine years. He was first appointed in 1947. In 1976, he was appointed district superintendent in the California-Nevada Conference.

10. On June 20, 1947, L. L. White transferred to the Southern California-Arizona Conference. He was appointed to the Holman Church in Los Angeles. He served this church for twenty-seven years. In 1974, he was appointed district superintendent of the Pasadena District.

11. The Saint Mark Church, New York City, was served by the Reverend W. H. Brooks for twenty-six years. He was first appointed in 1897. He retired in 1923. He died May 23, 1923.

12. One associate pastor merits citation in this regard. The Reverend Benjamin J. Haynes served the Jewella Charge of the Louisiana Conference for a quarter of a century. He was first appointed in 1949. He retired in 1974. He died December, 1975.

13. The members of the Metropolitan Community Church, New York City, have been served by the Reverend William James for twenty-six years. He was first appointed as the Senior Minister in 1952.

14. The Reverend Robert Moton Williams served the Asbury Church, Washington, D. C., for twenty-four years. He was first appointed in 1931. In 1955, he was

appointed as district superintendent of the Washington District. He died July 23, 1956.

15. The Gordon Memorial Church, Nashville, Tennessee, was served by the Reverend H. P. Gordon for twenty-four years as well. He was first appointed in 1923. In 1947, he was appointed to the Memphis District, Tennessee Conference. He died July 7, 1963.

16. The Reverend Charles L. Carrington was appointed to to the Brooks Memorial Church, Jamaica, New York, for twenty-three years. He was first appointed in 1941. He died March 3, 1965.

17. For twenty-three years, the Reverend J. W. Robinson served the Saint Mark Church, Chicago, Illinois. He was first appointed in 1899. He died November 27, 1941.

18. The Reverend Walter Scott Taylor was first appointed to the Galilee Church, Englewood, New Jersey in 1953. In respect for his leadership role, Englewood citizens elected him as their Mayor in 1971.

19. The Wier Charge of the Upper Mississippi Conference was served by the Reverend Donaldson Greene for twenty-two years. He was first appointed in 1905. He died September 17, 1950.

20. The Reverend Aaron D. Hall has served the Ebenezer Church at Miami, Florida for twenty-three years. He was first appointed in 1955.

21. The Reverend Joshua E. Licorish has served the oldest continuing black congregation for twenty-two years. He was first assigned to the Zoar Church, Philadelphia, Pennsylvania, in 1956.

22. The Mount Pleasant Church, Gainesville, Florida, has been served by the Reverend William Ferguson for twenty-two years. He was first appointed in 1956.

Biographical Sketches of Black Bishops

The first blacks to be elected to the episcopacy were missionary bishops. There were four missionary bishops elected for Liberia. In contrast to general superintendents, their authority was limited to Liberia only.

FRANCIS BURNS

The first black missionary bishop to be elected by the Methodist Episcopal Church was Francis Burns. He was elected by the Liberia Annual Conference in 1856. He was consecrated by Bishops Jane and Baker at the Genessee Conference on October 14, 1858.

He was born in Albany, New York, on December 5, 1809.[1] At the age of fifteen, he was converted and joined the Methodist Episcopal Church.

In 1833, he went to Liberia as a missionary. He served first as a teacher in Monrovia Seminary. He was appointed later as district superintendent of Cape Palmas District. He served as president of the Liberia Conference for six consecutive years. He served as missionary bishop for five years.

On April 18, 1863, he died in Baltimore, Maryland. In speaking about his ministry as the first black bishop, A. B. Hyde commented: "This first Methodist African bishop left a record as honorable as any of his white brethren."

JOHN WRIGHT ROBERTS

The second black missionary bishop was John Wright Roberts. He was born in Petersburg, Virginia on September 8, 1812.[2] He was the son of free parents.

His parents were very staunch members of the Methodist Episcopal Church. He joined the church in his early youth.

He went to Liberia as a missionary in 1838. He was admitted into the Liberia Conference in the same year. In 1841, he was elected to elder's orders.

He was elected as a missionary bishop in 1866. On June 20, 1866, he was consecrated by Bishops Scott and Jane.

The church flourished during his brief ministry in the episcopacy. The church was able to extend its ministry to adjacent regions. On Saturday, January 30, 1875, he died in Monrovia, Liberia.

ISAIAH BENJAMIN SCOTT

Almost thirty years passed before another missionary bishop was elected for Liberia. The third missionary bishop was Isaiah Benjamin Scott.

He was born in Woodford County, Kentucky on September 30, 1854. He was the youngest of fourteen children.

After the death of his father, the family moved to Austin, Texas.[3] He attended Clark University for his preparatory course. Upon completion of his high school course, he enrolled in Walden College for his baccalaureate degree. In 1876 he graduated.

After graduating from college, he served as pastor in Texas for several years. He served as a district superintendent of the Houston District. In 1893, he was elected as editor of the *Southwestern Christian Advocate*.

In 1904, he was elected missionary bishop for Liberia. He served as a missionary bishop for twelve years. He retired in 1916. On July 4, 1931, he died in Nashville, Tennessee.

ALEXANDER PRIESTLY CAMPHOR

The fourth and last of the black missionary bishops to Liberia was Alexander Priestly Camphor. He was born in a slave cabin on August 9, 1865, in New Orleans, Louisiana.

With the consent of his mother, he was adopted by the Reverend Stephen Priestly. After the adoption, Priestly was added as his middle name.

At fifteen, he left the public school and entered the preparatory school of New Orleans University. After he completed his high school course, he enrolled in New Orleans University. In 1889, he graduated with honors. In 1895, he graduated from Gammon Theological Seminary.

Upon graduating from the seminary, he went to Liberia as a missionary. For eleven years, he served as the president of the College of West Africa. For five years, he represented the United States as vice consul general to Liberia.

115

He returned to America in 1908. He was elected president of the Central Alabama Institute, Birmingham, Alabama. He held this position until he was elected missionary bishop. In 1916, he was elected missionary bishop to Liberia.[4]

His ministry as a missionary bishop was short indeed. On December 11, 1919, he died in Orange, New Jersey.

ROBERT ELIJAH JONES

The first general superintendent to be elected in the Methodist Episcopal Church was Robert Elijah Jones. He was the son of Sidney Dallas and Mary Jones. He was born in Greensboro, North Carolina on February 19, 1872.

In 1892, he was admitted on trial in the North Carolina Conference. In 1896, he was admitted into full connection and ordained an elder by Bishop Hurst.

He served only a brief span in the parish ministry. In 1897, he was elected as assistant manager of the *Southwestern Christian Advocate*. In 1901-1904, he served as field secretary of the Board of Sunday Schools. In 1904, he was elected editor of the *Southwestern Christian Advocate*. In this capacity, he remained until he was elected general superintendent.

On May 19, 1920, he was elected bishop on the first ballot.[5] He was assigned to the New Orleans Area. He served this area for four quadrennia. In 1936, he was assigned to the Columbus Area. He remained in this area until 1944.

He retired in 1944. He died on May 18, 1960. He was buried at Gulfside Assembly, Waveland, Mississippi.

MATTHEW WESLEY CLAIR, SR.

The second black general superintendent elected by the Methodist Episcopal Church was Matthew Wesley Clair, Sr. He was born in Union, West Virginia, on October 21, 1865. He was the son of Anthony and Mrs. Ollie Clair.

116

He was admitted into the Washington Conference in 1889. He was admitted into full connection in 1893 and ordained elder by Bishop Edward G. Andrews.

Before he was elected to the episcopacy, all his ministry was in the parish and as a district superintendent. He was appointed presiding elder in the Washington Conference in 1897. Again, he was appointed district superintendent of this district in 1919.

On May 20, 1920, he was elected bishop on the third ballot.[6] He was assigned to the Monrovia Area. In 1924, he was assigned to the Covington Area. He remained as the resident bishop until 1936. In 1936, he retired.

On June 25, 1943, he died in Covington, Kentucky. He was buried in Washington, D. C.

ALEXANDER PRESTON SHAW

The third black general superintendent elected by the Methodist Episcopal Church was Alexander Preston Shaw. He was the son of the Reverend Duncan and Mrs. Maria Shaw. He was born in Abbeville, Mississippi on April 18, 1879.

After graduating from Rust College and Gammon Seminary, he was admitted into the Washington Conference in 1908. He was admitted into full connection and ordained an elder by Bishop H. W. Warren in 1910.

He served twenty-three years in the Parish Ministry. In 1931, he was elected editor of the *Southwestern Christian Advocate*. He served as editor for five years.

On May 14, 1936, Alexander Preston Shaw was elected bishop in the Methodist Episcopal Church on the fifth ballot.[7] He was assigned to the New Orleans Area. In 1940, he was assigned to the newly created Baltimore Area. He remained here until he retired.

In 1952, he retired. On March 7, 1966, he died in Los Angeles, California. He was the last black bishop to be elected by the Methodist Episcopal Church.

WILLIAM ALFRED CARROLL HUGHES

The first bishop to be elected by the Methodist Church was William Alfred Carroll Hughes. He was born at Westminster, Maryland, June 19, 1877. He was the son of the Reverend and Mrs. Singleton Hughes.

He was admitted into the Washington Conference on trial in 1897. In 1900, he was admitted into full connection and ordained elder by Bishop H. H. Warren.

After he had served nine years in the pastorate, he was appointed a district superintendent. He served as a district superintendent for four years. In 1917, he was appointed as the field secretary of the Board of Home Missions and Church Extension.

On June 20, 1940, he was elected bishop on the second ballot by the first Central Jurisdictional Conference.[8] He was assigned to the New Orleans Area.

He died July 12, 1940. His ministry in the episcopacy was the shortest in historic Methodism.

LORENZO HOUSTON KING

The second Mississippian to be elevated to the episcopacy was Lorenzo Houston King. He was born in Macon, Mississippi on January 2, 1878. He was the son of Houston and Leah King.

After the completion of his college work at Clark University and Seminary work at Gammon Seminary, he was admitted into the Atlanta Conference on December 17, 1901. He was admitted into full connection and ordained elder by Bishop Luther B. Wilson in 1905.

His first appointment was the Elberton Charge. He served twenty-one years in the Pastorate. He served also as a professor at Clark University for one year. For ten years, he served as the courageous editor of the *Southwestern Christian Advocate*.

On June 21, 1940, he was elected bishop by the Central Jurisdictional Conference on the fifth ballot.[9] He was not a members of the Central Jurisdiction. He was assigned to the Atlantic Coast Area.

On December 17, 1946, he died in New York. He died on the forty-fifth anniversary of his admission to the Atlanta Conference on trial. He was the first bishop to be elected by a jurisdictional conference of which he was not a member.

WILLIS JEFFERSON KING

The third elder to be elected bishop by the Central Jurisdictional Conference was Willis Jefferson King. He was born in Rose Hill, Texas on October 1, 1886. He was the son of Anderson and Emma King.

Upon graduation from Wiley College and Boston School of Theology, he was admitted on trial in the Texas Conference in 1908. He was admitted into full connection and ordained elder by Bishop Hamilton in 1913.

After he had served in the parish ministry for eight years, his service record included college administration, professor of Old Testament at Gammon Seminary. From 1932 to 1944, he served as president of Gammon Seminary.

On June 9, 1944, he was elected bishop on the first ballot by the Central Jurisdictional Conference.[10]

He was assigned to the Monrovia Area for twelve years. In 1956, he was assigned to the New Orleans Area.

In 1960, he retired. He died in New Orleans, Louisiana on June 17, 1976. He was buried in Atlanta, Georgia.

ROBERT NATHANIEL BROOKS

The second bishop to be elected by the 1944 Central Jurisdictional Conference was Robert Nathaniel Brooks. He

119

was born in Hollis, North Carolina on May 8, 1888. He was the son of John and Louvenia Brooks.

After he had graduated from Bennett College and Gammon Seminary, he was admitted into the North Carolina Conference on trial in 1913. He was admitted into full connection and ordained an elder by Bishop E. H. Hughes in 1917.

He served in the Parish Ministry for two years. In 1918, he was appointed as Field Secretary of the Board of Sunday Schools. He served as president of three colleges. In 1926, he was elected professor of Church History at Gammon Seminary. He was elected editor of the *Southwestern Christian Advocate* in 1936.

On June 9, 1944, he was elected bishop on the third ballot.[11] He was assigned to the New Orleans Area for residential and presidential supervision. He served this area until his death.

On August 2, 1953, he died at Gulfside Assembly, Waveland, Mississippi.

EDWARD WENDELL KELLY

The second native Texan to be elected to the episcopacy was Edward Wendell Kelly. He was born in Mexia, Texas on December 27, 1880. He was the son of Taylor and Laura Kelly.

On December 19, 1912, he was admitted into the Texas Conference on trial. In 1916, he was admitted into full connection and was ordained elder by Bishop Thirkield.

He served twenty-nine years in the pastorate. He was elected bishop from the Union Memorial Church, Saint Louis, Missouri.

On June 10, 1944, he was elected bishop on the fifth ballot.[12] He served the Saint Louis Area until he retired.

In 1952, he retired. He died July 28, 1964, in Detroit, Michigan.

John Wesley Edward Bowen, Jr.

The Reverend John Wesley Bowen, Jr. was the son of the Reverend J. W. E. and Mrs. Ariel Serena Bowen, Sr. He was born in Baltimore, Maryland on September 24, 1889.

In 1917, he was admitted into the Atlanta Conference on trial. He was admitted into full connection and was ordained elder by Bishop McDowell in 1919.

His first appointment was as an instructor at Walden College. For two years he served as a chaplain in the United States Army. On release, he served as field agent for the board of Sunday Schools for three years. He then returned to the classroom as an instructor at Claflin College.

From 1925 to 1936, he served in the pastorate. In 1936, he was appointed district superintendent of the New Orleans District. After completion of his term on the district, he was appointed pastor of First Street Church. In 1944, he was elected editor of the *Central Christian Advocate.*

On June 11, 1948, he was elected bishop on the third ballot.[13] He was assigned to the Atlantic Coast Area. He remained here as resident bishop until he retired.

In 1960, he retired. On July 12, 1962, he died in Atlanta, Georgia.

Edgar Amos Love

The third black bishop to be elected from the Washington Conference was Edgar Amos Love. The Reverend Edgar Love was the son of the Reverend Julius C. and Susie K. Love. He was born September 10, 1891 in Harrisonburg, Virginia.

He was admitted on trial in the Washington Conference in 1915. In 1917, he was admitted into full connection and ordained an elder by Bishop McDowell.

He served for two years as chaplain in the United States Army. Upon release he served as an instructor at Morgan College for one year. From 1921 to 1933, he served in the pastorate. He was appointed district superintendent of the Washington District in 1934. Upon completion of his term, he was elected superintendent of Negro work of the Board of Missions.

On June 20, 1952, he was elected on the third ballot.[14] He was assigned to the Baltimore Area. He remained as the resident bishop until he retired. In 1964, he retired. On May 1, 1974, he died in Baltimore, Maryland.

MATTHEW WALKER CLAIR, JR.

The second bishop to be elected by the 1952 Central Jurisdictional Conference was Matthew Walker Clair, Jr. He was unique among his peers. He was the son of a bishop.

He was the son of the Reverend Matthew Walker and Fannie Clair. He was born to this union at Harper's Ferry, Virginia, on August 12, 1891.

He was admitted on trial in the Washington Conference in 1915. He was admitted into full connection and ordained an elder by Bishop McDowell in 1918.

After a brief span of two years in the pastorate, he served as a chaplain in the United States Army. Upon release from his army duties, he served sixteen years in the parish ministry. In 1936, he was elected professor of Practical Theology at Gammon Seminary. After he had served four years, he returned to the parish ministry. He was appointed to the Saint Mark's Church, Chicago, Illinois, for twelve years.

On June 20, 1952, he was elected bishop by the Central Jurisdictional Conference on the fourth ballot.[15] He was assigned to the Saint Louis Area.

In 1964, he retired. On July 10, 1968, he died in Saint Louis, Missouri.

PRINCE ALBERT TAYLOR, JR.

The only elder to be elected bishop in historic Methodism from Oklahoma is Prince Albert Taylor, Jr. He is the son of the Reverend Prince Albert and Bertha Taylor, Sr. He was born in Hennessay, Oklahoma on January 27, 1907.

In 1929, he was admitted on trial in the North Carolina Conference. He was admitted in full connection and ordained an elder by Bishop Wallace A. Brown in 1931.

From 1931 to 1940, he served four charges. He was elected assistant to the president of Bennett College in 1940. In 1944, he was elected professor of Christian Education at Gammon Seminary. He was elected editor of the *Central Christian Advocate* in 1948.

On June 16, 1956, he was elected bishop on the ninth ballot.[16] He was assigned to the Monrovia Area for two quadrennia. In 1964, he was assigned to the New Jersey Area. He served three quadrennia. On July 15, 1976, he retired.

He was the first black general superintendent to serve as the president of the Council of Bishops. He was the president for 1966.

CHARLES FRANKLIN GOLDEN

The sixth Central Jurisdictional Conference elected three general superintendents. The Reverend Charles Franklin Golden was the first to be elected.

He is the son of the Reverend James Walter and Mary Golden. He was born in Holly Springs, Mississippi, on August 24, 1912.

In 1934, he was admitted into the Upper Mississippi Conference on trial. He was admitted in full connection by Bishop A. P. Shaw in 1938.

He was assigned to Clarksdale Charge. After serving a few months, he was transferred to the Southwest Conference and appointed to the Wesley Church, Little Rock, Arkansas. In 1942, he was appointed as chaplain in the United States Army. After his release from this tour of duty, he was elected to the Board of Missions in 1947. He served thirteen years in this position.

On July 14, 1960, he was elected bishop on the third ballot.[17] He was assigned to the Nashville-Birmingham Area for 1960-1964. In 1964 he was assigned to the Carolina Area. In 1968, he was assigned bishop of the San Francisco Area in the Western Jurisdiction. In 1972, he was assigned by the Western Jurisdictional Conference to the Los Angeles Area. He was returned to this Area at the 1976 Jurisdictional Conference.

NOAH WATSON MOORE, JR.

The Delaware Conference was honored by the Central Jurisdictional Conference in 1960. One of its sons was elevated to the episcopacy. The Reverend Noah Watson Moore, Jr. was elected bishop.

He is the son of the Reverend Noah Watson and Mrs. Eliza Moore, Sr. He was born in Newark, New Jersey on March 28, 1902.

The Delaware Conference admitted him on trial in 1930. He was admitted into full connection and ordained as elder by Bishop E. G. Richardson in 1932.

His first appointment was New Rochelle, New York. With the exception of two years as a district Superintendent of the Eastern District, all his ministry was in the pastorate. He served twenty-eight years in the parish ministry. His last appointment before his election to the episcopacy was Tindley Temple Church, Philadelphia, Pennsylvania. He served this church for eleven years.

On July 14, 1960, he was elected bishop by the Central Jurisdictional Conference on the fourth ballot.[18] He was assigned to the New Orleans Area. When the Central Jurisdiction was abolished, he was assigned to the Nebraska Area in 1968. In 1972, he retired.

Marquis Lafayette Harris

The third bishop to be elected by the 1960 Central Jurisdictional Conference was Marquis Lafayette Harris. He was born in Armstrong, Alabama, on March 8, 1907. He was the son of William Eugene and Estella Harris.

The Lexington Conference admitted him on trial in 1930. In 1932, he was admitted into full connection and ordained an elder by Bishop M. W. Clair, Sr.

He served three years in the pastorate. The remaining of his ministry was in college administration. He served as dean of Samuel Houston College for three years. In 1936, he was elected president of Philander Smith College. He served in this capacity for fourteen years.

On July 15, 1960, he was elected bishop by the Central Jurisdictional Conference on the tenth ballot.[19] He was assigned to the Atlantic Coast Area. He served in the office of episcopacy for six years.

On October 7, 1966, he died in Atlanta, Georgia.

James Samuel Thomas, Jr.

The 1964 Central Jurisdictional Conference elected one bishop. It elected James Samuel Thomas.

He is a native of Orangeburg, South Carolina. He was born April 8, 1919. He is the son of the Reverend Samuel and Dessie Thomas, Sr.

The South Carolina Conference admitted him on trial in 1942. In 1945, he was admitted in full connection and ordained an elder by Bishop Willis J. King.

He served two years in the parish ministry. For one year he served as chaplain of the South Carolina State College. In 1947, he was elected as professor of Rural Church at Gammon Seminary. The Board of Education elected him as staff member in 1953. He remained in this position until his elevation to the episcopacy.

On July 19, 1964, he was elected bishop on the seventeenth ballot.[20] He was transferred to the North Central Jurisdiction and was assigned as the resident bishop of the Iowa Area.

In 1976, he was assigned to the Ohio East Area for presidential and residential supervision.

Bishop Thomas was the first black general superintendent to deliver the Episcopal Address at a General Conference. He delivered this address at the 1976 General Conference.

LINUENT SCOTT ALLEN

The last bishop to be elected by the Central Jurisdictional Conference was Linuent Scott Allen. The Magnolia State has led in the production of black bishops.

He is a native Mississippian. He was born in Meridian, Mississippi on May 8, 1918. He is the son of Louis and Mabel Allen.

The Atlanta Conference admitted him on trial in 1938. In 1942, he was admitted in full connection and ordained an elder by Bishop R. E. Jones.

Prior to his election as editor of the *Central Christian Advocate,* he served sixteen years in the Parish Ministry. In 1956, he left the Central Church, Atlanta to assume editorship of the *Central Christian Advocate.* He was editor for eleven years.

On August 18, 1967, he was elected bishop on the second ballot.[21] He was assigned to the Gulf Coast Area. In 1968, he was assigned by the Southeastern Jurisdictional Conference to the Holston Area. In 1976, he was assigned to the Western North Carolina Area.

ROY CALVIN NICHOLS

The first black to be elected by a regional jurisdiction was Roy Calvin Nichols. He was elected by the Northeastern Jurisdiction.

126

The Reverend Roy Calvin Nichols is the son of Roy and Mamie Nichols. He was born in Hurlock, Maryland on March 19, 1918.

The California-Nevada Conference admitted him on trial in 1949. He was admitted in full connection and ordained an elder by Bishop Donald Tippett in 1951.

All his ministry prior to his election to the episcopacy was in the Parish Ministry. He served the Downs Church, Oakland, California, 1949–1964. In 1964, he was transferred to the New York Conference and appointed to the Salem Church. Here he served until he was elected bishop in the United Methodist Church.

On July 26, 1968, Roy C. Nichols was elected bishop by the Northeastern Jurisdiction on the fourteenth ballot.[22] He was assigned to the Pittsburgh Area for residential and presidential supervision. He was reassigned in 1972 and 1976.

EDWARD GONZALES CARROLL

The second black elder to be elevated to the episcopacy from the Northeastern Jurisdiction was Edward Gonzales Carroll. He is a native of West Virginia. He was born on January 7, 1910, in Wheeling, West Virginia. He is the son of Julius Sylvester and Florence Carroll.

In 1933, he was admitted into the Washington Conference on trial. In 1935, he was admitted into full connection and ordained an elder by Bishop Edwin Holt Hughes.

He served ten years in the pastorate. His first appointment was Mount Washington and Salem. He served as a chaplain in the United States Army from 1942 to 1945. From 1945 to 1950, he served as a Y.M.C.A. Secretary. From 1961-1967, he served as the district superintendent of the Washington District. His last appointment before he was elected to the episcopacy was the Marvin Memorial Church, an inclusive but predominantly white congregation, in suburban Washington, D. C.

On July 12, 1972, the Northeastern Jurisdictional Conference elected him as General Superintendent on the ninth ballot.[23] He was assigned to the Boston Area. In 1976, he was reassigned to the Boston Area.

ERNEST THOMAS DIXON

The first black elder to be elected bishop by the South Central Jurisdiction was Ernest Thomas Dixon. He is a native Texan. He was born in San Antonio, Texas on October 13, 1922. He is the son of Ernest Thomas and Ethel Dixon.

The West Texas Conference admitted him on trial on October 15, 1943. He was admitted to full connection and ordained an elder by Bishop Robert N. Brooks in 1946.

His service record reveals that all his ministry has been extra-parish ministry. From 1945–1951, he served on the faculty of Tuskeegee Institute. In 1952, he served as executive secretary of Christian Education of the West Texas Conference. In 1953, he was appointed staff member of the Board of Education. In 1965, he was elected president of Philander Smith College.

In 1968, he served as a staff member of the Program Council of the Church. On July 12, 1972, the South Central Jurisdictional Conference elected him bishop on the ninth ballot.[24] He was assigned to the Kansas Area. In 1976, he was reassigned to that area.

EDSEL ALBERT AMMONS

The first black bishop to be elected by the North Central Jurisdiction was Edsel A. Ammons. He is the son of Albert Clifton and Lila Kay Ammons. He was born February 17, 1924, in Chicago, Illinois.

He was admitted in the Rock River Conference as a traveling elder in full connection from the A.M.E. Church in 1957.

128

His first appointment in the Methodist Church was Whitfield. He served this charge for two years. In 1959, he was appointed to the Ingleside Whitfield Parish. He served for three years. From 1963–1966, he served as the director of urban work on the Rockford District. In 1961, he was elected to the staff of the Conference Program Council. He served two years. In 1968, he was appointed professor at Garrett-Evangelical Theological Seminary.

On July 15, 1976, he was elected bishop on the eighteenth ballot. He was assigned to the Michigan Area.

Leadership Roles in General Board and on the Conference Level

Prior to 1964, there were only a few black staff members in the General Boards of the Church. Most of those serving were field agents of the Boards.

The first Negro to serve as a corresponding secretary of a general board was Madison B. Mason. He was the corresponding secretary of the Freedmen's Aid and Southern Education Society. He was elected in 1896 and served until 1912.

The Committee of Five of the Central Jurisdiction sent a memorial to the General Conference requesting that the General Conference would authorize boards and agencies to establish an open door policy regarding the employment of staff. The General Conference approved of the memorial. Competence became the qualification without regard to race, color or sex.

Since 1964, blacks are no longer serving in honorific positions. They are now serving as staff members at the decision-making level. Two Blacks have been elected as general secretaries of two boards. The Reverend Melvin Talbert of the Southern California-Arizona Conference was elected general secretary of the Board of Discipleship in 1972. In 1976, the Reverend George Outen, Eastern Pennsylvania

Conference, was elected as general secretary of the Board of Church and Society.

Two associate general secretaries of the Board of Global Ministries are the Reverend Randolph Nugent and Miss Theresa Hoover. The Reverend John Norwood of the North Alabama Conference is an associate general secretary in the Council of Finance and Administration. The Reverend Ernest Smith of the North Mississippi Conference is an associate secretary of the Board of Church and Society. In 1976, Mr. Leonard Miller of Philadelphia, Pennsylvania, was elected as an associate secretary of the General Council on Ministries. Readus J. Watkins, associate general secretary of the Division of Program and Benevolence Interpretation, United Methodist Communications, assumed office in July, 1977.

Two other blacks must be included in decision making at the highest level. The Reverend W. Talbot Handy, Jr. of the Louisiana Conference has been serving as vice-president of the United Methodist Publishing House since 1970. The Reverend Woodie White of the Detroit Conference is the executive secretary of the Commission of Religion and Race.

There are four black ministers serving as council directors. The following ministers are serving as top executives in the following conferences: Anthony Shipley, Detroit Conference; Forrest Stith, Baltimore Conference; Willie B. Clay, Northern Illinois Conference and Luther W. Henry of the Central Texas Conference. There are also thirty black ministers serving as district superintendents.

Leadership of Black Americans in the Mission Field

During the first decade of the twentieth century, Georgia sent two dedicated women to the mission field. They were Martha Drummer of Barnesville, Georgia, and Anna Hall of Bainbridge, Georgia.

Upon graduation from Clark University in 1901, Miss

Drummer continued her training at the Northeastern Deaconess Training School in Boston, Massachusetts. She specialized in nurse training.

In 1906, she sailed for Angola, Portuguese West Africa. She spent sixteen years in Africa in ministering to the bodies and souls of the Africans. In speaking of ministry, Karl Downs wrote, "From this saintly woman, many a despondent shipwrecked person found a true gem of hope."

In 1922, she retired from missionary service. On December 11, 1937, Miss Drummer died in Atlanta, Georgia. Her dying words: "Say Africa when you pray."

On December 15, 1901, Miss Anna Hall was consecrated as a deaconess by Bishop J. M. Walden in Newnan, Georgia. She was the first black to be be consecrated as a Deaconess in the Methodist Episcopal Church.[25]

She sailed for Liberia in 1906. On arrival, Bishop Camphor assigned here as principal of the Krootown School. During her first year, she conducted a revival. More than three hundred persons were converted. For twenty-five years, she expended herself in the Cause of Christ. She described it in these words: "For twenty-five years, I gave my life for service and sacrifice." On July 1, 1932, she retired. She continued her missionary work at the Central Church in Atlanta. On March 6, 1964, Miss Hall died here.

In 1948, the Reverend Ulysses and Mrs. Vivian Gray were commissioned as missionaries. They were assigned to Liberia.

On arrival in Liberia, they were appointed to the College of West Africa. After a brief period, they were moved to the United Methodist Mission in Gbarnga. They served here for a quarter of a century.

At Gbarnga, Mrs. Gray established the first school to be approved by the Department of Public Instruction. It was approved in February, 1949. The school began in Mud Chapel with seventy-three pupils in the first three grades. In 1959, the course of study was extended to six grades.

The Reverend Gray divided his ministry between the

131

parish and as an agricultural missionary. He taught people new methods in crop production. Many were added to the church by the preaching of the word and exemplary examples of their Christian lives.

They inspired many young Africans during their stay in Liberia. They influenced the lives of Mrs. Minerva Nagbe, the wife of the late Bishop Stephen Nagbe and Bishop Warner, the resident bishop of Liberia.

On July 26, 1974, President William R. Talbert, Jr., of Liberia, conferred the Liberian distinction of Knight Commander upon the Reverend Gray. On the same day, he conferred the Grand Band of the Order of the Star of Africans upon Mrs. Vivian Gray. These honors were conferred upon this unselfish missionary couple on the occasion of the 127th Independence Day Celebration of the Nation of Liberia. They retired in 1975.

Another missionary couple made history in the missionary movement, Thomas and Jennie Harris of Florida. They were commissioned in 1948 and assigned to China. Their first assignment was to the Fukien Province. Here they studied Mandarin in preparation of their tasks as agricultural missionaries. Their stay here was cut short by the curtailment of their work by communist rule.

In 1951, this missionary couple was assigned to Sarawak, a British Crown Colony. They were located 170 miles in interior Sarawak, Northwest Coast of Borneo. Their ministry was among the Iba Tribesmen. Some of these tribesmen had practiced head-hunting as recently as World War II. They were called the "Jungle Missionaries." Here they made their witness for Christ and His Church in the most perilous situations.

The Reverend Tunnie Martin, native of Orangeburg, South Carolina, was commissioned as a missionary to India. In 1949, he was appointed as a teacher in the Christian High School at Jabalpar M.P. Later, he was made principal. In this position, he served until 1961. In addition to his teaching responsibility, he served as a rural extension worker at the

United Christian School at Jullundur. In 1962, he became the manager of Ranikhet Mission Intermediate College. He served also as the district superintendent of the Bareilly District.

Black Methodists in Ecumenical Roles

The Mother Methodist Church has always had a tolerant spirit toward other branches of the Christian faith. Some black Methodist have made their witness in ecumenical circles.

The American Bible Society is an organization that is ecumenical in nature. In 1901, J. P. Wragg, Atlanta Conference, was elected as Superintendent of the Colored work of the American Bible Society. He retired in 1931. His successor was Daniel H. Stanton, Atlanta Conference. He served for 25 years. He died June 18, 1957.

The Interdenominational Theological Center was organized in Atlanta, Georgia in 1959. It was a cooperative ecumenical venture of four denominations. Its first president was Harry V. Richardson, Central Alabama Conference. He retired in 1969. The Reverend Oswald P. Bronson, Georgia Conference, was elected as his successor. In 1975, he resigned as president. The third president is Dr. Grant Shockley of the Holston Conference.

Civic Roles of Black Methodists

Increasingly, black Methodists are playing significant leadership roles in society. The shortest list of outstanding Black Methodists as civil servants must include Mary McLeod Bethune. In 1932, Ida Tarbell, the journalist, included her in the list of the "Fifty Greatest Women in American History." She was a native of South Carolina.

She began her life with an affirmation—"that no obstacle cannot be overcome by the strength of spirit and power of will." Her achievements as a civil servant may be attributed to her determined will.

133

Her early ambition was to go to Africa as a missionary. She was rejected as a missionary by the Presbyterian Board. Like Paul, she was "perplexed but not in despair." Instead, she went to Daytona Beach, Florida and established a college for girls. The school was opened in 1903 with a dream and one dollar and fifty cents. As evidence of her faith, the first building erected was called Faith Hall.

It was her conviction that the use of the ballot box was one of the best means of achieving equal rights for her people. Despite the fear technique used by the Klu Klux Klan, she led a group of her teachers to the voting booth. They refused to leave until they were permitted to vote.

On June 28, 1935, Mrs. Bethune was awarded the Joel E. Spingarn Gold Medal by the National Association for the Advancement of Colored People. In the citation, she was praised for her courage in speaking against, as well as working to remove, the racial barriers against her people.

On December 5, 1935, she was the prime organizer of the National Council of Negro Women. Its purpose was to articulate action of Negro women in a federation of a national women's organization.

President Roosevelt appointed her to serve on the Advisory Board of the National Youth Administration. One of her responsibilities was to report directly to the president. On one occasion, she closed her report to the president with these words:

> Blacks are in quest for full citizenship. We have been eating the crumbs long enough. We want bread now.

In 1945, Mrs. Bethune was appointed by President Truman as an official consultant to draft the Charter for the United Nations. She was the only black woman in the delegation with official status.

In appreciation for her long and arduous labors in the field of human relations, Rollins College conferred upon her the Doctor of Humanities on February 22, 1949. It is reputed that this was the first time that a college in the Deep South had honored a Negro.

On May 17, 1955, this octogenarian died. She was a millionaire, not in stocks and bonds, but in the number of black youths who had been inspired by her as a civic leader.

A Negro poet who won civic acclamation was Countee Cullen. He was the adopted son of the Reverend Frederick Asbury and Mrs. Carolyn Belle Cullen. He grew up in Salem Methodist Episcopal Church in New York.

During the 1920s, he was very active in the Harlem-centered Negro Renaissance. He strove to awaken within the Negroes an appreciation for their black heritage. At the same time, he expressed his protest to the inequalities in American Society. He broke through the racial barriers in both the academic and publishing circles. In his first book, *Caroling Dusk,* he used his pen to break the insuperable barriers of his people. In these words, he expressed his protest against discrimination:

> She even thinks that up in Heaven
> Her class lies and
> snores
> While poor black cheribs rise at
> Seven
> To do the celestial chores.

Another outstanding civic leader is Clarence M. Mitchell. He is a trusteee and member of the Sharp Street Church, Baltimore, Maryland.

He distinguished himself as a lawyer early. In 1933, he gave testimony before a Senate committee in investigating lynching. He is a member of the United States delegation to the United Nations.

In 1969, he became a Spingarn Medalist. The citation included this statement:

For his selfless devotion to the task of ending social bias;
For his uncompromising rejection of racism, White or
Black . . . for his abiding faith in the democratic process
as a means of achieving freedom and equality for all.

In the field of music, Leontyne Price has been an outstanding civic servant. She is a native of Laurel, Mississippi. She was reared in the Saint Paul United Methodist Church.

After much striving, she became a Metropolitan Opera singer. In recognition of her divinely inspired talent, in tribute to extraordinary achievement as the outstanding soprano of the era, and in appreciation of her priceless contributions as an artist, citizen, and person to the continuing crusade for justice, equality, and understanding among the peoples of the world, she was awarded the Spingarn Medal on January 2, 1966.

Gloster Bryant Current has distinguished himself in his fight for equal rights for all people. He is the Director of Branches and Field Administration of the National Association for the Advancement of Colored People. He has administrative responsibility for 1700 branches in fifty states. He has served in this capacity since 1946. He is a charter member of the Saint Paul Church, Jamaica, New York, where he is the associate minister. He is always on hand to make his social witness in this church.

Another laywoman merits inclusion in the enumeration of outstanding civic leaders. This laywoman, Clarie Collins Harvey, is from Jackson, Mississippi, and a member of the Central United Methodist Church.

From 1972–1974, she served as the president of the Church Women United. In 1974, she received the churchwoman of the year award from the Religious Heritage of America. Three years earlier, the Jackson City Council awarded her the outstanding citizen award. During the same year, Governor William Waller declared December 30, 1971, "Clarie Collins Harvey Day."

The Mississippi Delta town, Clarksdale, has been blessed

in the civic role ascription of Aaron Henry. During the crisis period in the state, Mr. Henry emerged as the civil rights hero. He is a firm believer that the ballot box is an instrument by which many of the wrongs in society can be corrected. He has encouraged blacks to register and vote.

He is the president of the Mississippi Chapter of the National Association for the Advancement of Colored People. He is an active member of the Haven United Methodist Church.

Leadership Roles of Black Methodists in Political Life

Black Methodists have participated minimally in politics since the Reconstruction Period. They have engaged in politics on the national, state, and local level.

The earliest black Methodist to earn national acclaim was Hiram Rhodes Revels. The Reverend Revels was a native of Fayetteville, North Carolina. He was a member of the Mississippi Conference. He was the first black to be seated in the Congress of the United States. He was elected to fill the unexpired term of Jefferson Davis in the Senate.

There was strong opposition in the Senate to seating him. After hours of animated debate, the Senate voted forty-eight for and eight against his admission. On Friday, February 25, 1870, he took the Oath of Office at 4:40 P.M.[26]

Revels had a very short tenure in the Senate. His term expired in 1871. In the Senate, he was a voice of moderation of race relations. He supported the bill for the general removal of political disabilities of Southern whites. He succeeded in obtaining the admission of Negro mechanics to work in United States Navy yards.

At least one outstanding black laywoman has been elected to the United States House of Representatives in the twentieth century. On November 5, 1968, Mrs. Shirley Anita Chisholm, Brooklyn, New York, was elected to the House of Representatives by the 12th District. Because of her courageous leadership, she has been reelected to the 92nd, 93rd, 94th, and 95th Congresses.

She came to this position with a wealth of experience in the political field. She was an assemblywoman of the New York Legislature for four years.

Mrs. Chisholm is an active member of Jones United Methodist Church in Brooklyn, New York.

Special mention must be made of Perry Wilborn Howard. From 1921 to 1929, he served as the Assistant to the Attorney General of the United States. Attorney Howard was a native of Ebenezer, Mississippi. He was a graduate of Rust College. He was a member of the Asbury Methodist Episcopal Church, Washington, D. C.

Mrs. Anna Hedgeman served in the United States Department of Health, Education and Welfare as an assistant to the administrator. She served as the executive director of the National Council for Permanent Fair Employment Practices Commission, 1944–1946. In 1953, she was an exchange leader of the State Department to India. She is a native of Iowa, and a member of the Saint Mark United Methodist Church, New York City.

In addition to those leaders on the national level, there have been several blacks who fulfilled important roles on the state level. The Reverend Henry Cardoza was a state senator of South Carolina. He served in the Senate from Kershaw County from 1870–1874. He was a member of the South Carolina Conference.

During the Reconstruction Period, the Reverend A. K. Davis served as Lieutenant Governor of Mississippi from 1874 until his impeachment in 1875. He was cleared of his impeachment charges in criminal court. He was a member of the Mississippi Conference.

At least one black Methodist served as the secretary of the state. The Reverend James D. Lynch served as the secretary of the state of Mississippi. His career in politics was short-lived. He died on December 18, 1872, in Jackson, Mississippi. He was buried in Greenwood Cemetery on

December 20, 1872. In appreciation of his arduous labors, the legislature authorized an appropriation for a monument in his memory.

During the recent years, at least four black Methodists have been elected to state houses. The Reverend Zan Holmes, Jr., served in the Texas State House from 1968 to 1972. He was the State Representative from District 33, Place 5, Dallas County. He is a member of the Southwest Texas Conference.

The 93rd Louisiana Legislative District elected Mrs. Dorothy Mae Taylor as a state legislator in 1972. She is a member of the Mount Zion United Methodist Church, New Orleans, Louisiana.

The Reverend Marion Daniel Bennett, a native of South Carolina, was elected as a state assemblyman for Nevada in 1973. He is a member of the Southern-California, Arizona Conference. He is the pastor of Zion United Methodist Church, Las Vegas, Nevada.

Some black Methodists have achieved significant leadership roles on the local level. The mayor of Compton, California, is Doris Davis. She is a member of the Wesley United Methodist Church, Los Angeles, California.

The Reverend W. R. Crawford was one of the first blacks to be elected as an alderman for Winston-Salem, North Carolina. He was elected in 1955 and served until 1961. He was also a member of the school board. He is a member of Western North Carolina Conference.

In addition to serving as pastor of the Union Memorial Church, Saint Louis, Missouri, the Reverend John Josephus Hicks served on the Saint Louis School Board from 1959 to 1964. He is now serving on the Community School Board, District V, of New York City. He is a member of the New York Conference. He is now the pastor in charge of the Saint Mark United Methodist Church in New York City.

CHAPTER IX

Black United Methodists in Prospect

In Chapter VII, *de facto* inclusiveness on the associative level was described. Legislation was the procedural method of achieving this proximate goal. On this level, relationships are secondary. Hence, *de facto* inclusiveness was less difficult in achieving. But on the communal or local church level, relationships are primary and intimate. Legislation will not achieve *de facto* inclusiveness on this level.

The real test of an inclusive fellowship must be measured by the quality of interpersonal relations at this level. The real strength of the church is found in the quality of Christian life lived and taught in the local church.

The real question facing the United Methodist Church is not how to achieve total inclusiveness on the local church level. Rather, it should be what is the future of the black people in the United Methodist fellowship? This question will be answered when the following questions have been answered:

(1) What about ministerial recruitment, training, and deployment of blacks?

(2) What about open itineracy for black ministers? Will they be frozen into same appointment for an indefinite period of time?

(3) Will the black preacher continue to be social prophets for his people? Will he or she have a "free pulpit"?

(4) What about membership growth?

(5) What about the leadership roles of blacks in the church?

(6) Does the program of the black church answer the basic needs of black people?

(7) Will the church be satisfied to guarantee to trained black ministers only the minimum salary of the conference?

(8) What about church facilities? Are they adequate?

(9) Will the church continue to advocate unity through diversity?

(10) Assuming that a local church serves all peoples in its primary service area, will the church work for open occupancy and residential desegregation?

These are typical questions which must be answered in order to project the future of black people in the United Methodist Church.

It is almost midnight. The church must plan now. It must plan for the future by purpose rather than default. The future is now.

The Local Church As the Witnessing Community

The local churches are the foundation stones on which the connectional system is built. Without the local churches, there would be no need for pastors, district superintendents, general boards or agencies, or even bishops. The right price tag must be placed again on the local church.

The primary emphasis must be placed upon the strengthening of the local churches in order that they may become real witnessing communities. According to the Discipline, "the local church is a community of true believers under the Lordship of Christ. . . . The local church is a strategic base from which Christians move out to the structures of society." (Paragraph 101–102) It is therefore all believers' responsibility to enable the local churches to be these in fact.

Ministerial Leadership

High on the agenda of the Church must be recruitment, training, and deployment of black ministers. Adequate supply of trained ministers is an absolute necessity in the empowering of local churches.

It is a sad commentary, but the ministerial supply for black churches has been reduced at an increasing rate for many years. From 1952 to 1961, the Central Jurisdictional Conferences admitted only 304 men and women into full connection. For the same decade, the Jurisdiction lost 522 ministers by death, withdrawal, expulsion, voluntary, or involuntary location.[1] In addition, 275 men were retired. For every one admitted into full connection, two terminated their effective relationship. In 1940, the median age of black ministers was 50.5 years. In 1961, it was 53.5 years.

From 1960 to 1964, all the seminaries graduated only 412 black men and two black ladies with the Bachelor of Divinity or its equivalent degree.[2] Only 108 were Black United Methodist.

The South Carolina Conference has been a seedbed for ministerial recruitment in the past. Almost every minister in the conference was a native. It developed indigenous leadership. It also had the highest number of seminary graduates among the black conferences. In 1962, it had 151 men in full connection. Its median age was 49.9 years, the lowest in the Jurisdiction. By 1975, the black ministers in the integrated South Carolina Conference had declined to 75 men in full connection and 11 men on probation. The median age was 53.2 years.

In his study: "Let's Get Acquainted," Dr. James H. Davis warned the New Peninsula Conference in these words:

The New Peninsula Conference must act within the next few years to reduce the number of (black) appointments, add more churches to some (black) charges, supply some black) congregations with white pastors, or recruit at least ten (black) pastors.[3]

Because this warning was not heeded, this conference now needs at least twenty new pastors to maintain the present charge alignments.

In 1954, this writer admonished the Central Jurisdiction leaders of this incipient plight. He warned that if this trend was not reversed, the Central Jurisdiction would be abolished by default. Ten years later, the General Conference had to pass enabling legislation to continue four black annual conferences. These conferences had fewer than fifty ministerial members.

Reasons can be given, explanations can be made, excuses can be offered, but the undeniable fact is that there has been a growing dearth of black ministerial leadership for a long time. Let no one assume that the abolition of the Central Jurisdiction is the reason. The malignant neglect of recruitment of black ministers has imperiled the black constituency of the church. Black ministerial leadership is now and will be for a long time necessary for increasing black memberships in the church.

There is always a great danger when the demands exceed the supply. Pulpits are often supplied with unqualified persons. Included in black church memberships are trained lay persons. The church can ill afford to appoint unqualified ministers to these churches.

In addition, the church must recruit trained black ministers if *de facto* inclusiveness on the local church level is to become a reality. Ministers must be qualified to move *horizontally* and *vertically*. Black ministers must not be granted "special qualifications"; instead, they should meet the same Disciplinary requirements as other ministers. However, they must not be required to "over-qualify" in order to become

143

regular itinerants in the United Methodist Ministry. Open itineracy must be the ultimate goal to which the Church must be striving.

Adequate financial assistance must be secured for this all important task. Scholarship assistance is needed for college training and seminary training. Increased giving to the Crusade Scholarship would help immeasurably. Other scholarship programs must receive more money as well. Conferences must also increase their support to ministerial education.

Free Pulpit

The church must maintain a free pulpit for all its ministers. The black ministers in the past were perforce to become the prophetic voices of their people. They must not be deprived of this role in integrated conferences.

As long as there are injustices in the society, as long as the strong continue to oppress the weak, as long as people are deprived of building a home where they choose, as long as there are discriminatory practices in the employment system, as long as there exists sex discrimination and locational discrimination, there must be a "prophetic voice" condemning these unChristian practices. If the black preachers remain unmuzzled, it will have a reciprocal effect in the white pulpits by freeing some of the white ministers from their enslavement.

In 1948, the Council of Bishops went on record affirming a free pulpit for all its ministers. In the Episcopal Address, Bishop G. Bromley Oxnam said:

> We are determined that free preachers occupying free pulpits, preaching to free laymen in a free land shall proclaim the freeing truth of the religion of Jesus . . . Methodism is determined not to allow the intimidation of its clergy. We call upon our laymen, whose freedom is equally involved to join with our preachers in maintaining this freedom in the presence of social systems that deny it.[4]

144

The Multiple Roles of Black Ministers

The role expectation of black people has been that the black ministers would serve them in all their relationships. The black preacher has in the past been a leader for his people in all their crisis situations. He has been the "generalist" because he was in many cases the only leader they had. Hence, the black minister has been ascribed multiple roles, e.g., pastor, preacher, teacher, counselor, civic leader, and community organizer. These roles were interlocking and mutually reciprocal.

The black minister must still encourage his people to register and vote. The ballot box is still one way to get redress from social wrongs inflicted upon black people. Black people are still being discriminated against in the economic field. The black preacher should continue his role as a community organizer against the cruel systems which are crushing his people.

Recruitment and Training of Lay Leadership

In order to survive the black church needs to aggressively recruit new members. The ratio of black members to total church membership is declining at an increasing rate. In 1799, Negroes constituted one-fifth of the total church membership. In 1843, black members constituted 12 percent of the total church membership. Today, there are 353,326 Blacks in the United Methodist Church, constituting 3.52 percent of the total church membership.

It is being reported today that black church membership in the United Methodist Church is declining at an increasing rate. If this is the case, concerted efforts should be made to discover the reasons for such drastic loss in church membership.

It is the assumption of this writer, however, that black church membership is not declining as rapidly as some assume, but that there is now more accurate reporting of church memberships.

Under the efficient leadership of Dr. Maceo Pembrooke, Saint Mark Church in Chicago led the way in removing inactive members. It took courage to do this because church leaders did not look with favor upon net membership loss. In its Fourth Quarterly Conference, April 29, 1963, this church dropped 875 members from its roll. This action was based upon paragraph 127 of the 1960 Discipline.

The Lexington Conference questioned the authority of this quarterly conference. It referred the matter to the Judicial Council for a ruling. On May 1, 1964, the Judicial Council ruled that the Saint Mark Church had complied with the Discipline of the church and the action of the quarterly conference was affirmed.[5] In 1967, this church continued its purging process. It dropped 1,727 members from its roll. Other churches have now taken similar actions.

In addition to the action of the judicial Council, black churches are now fully aware that membership is a factor in apportionment to charges. More churches are now attempting to bring their memberships in line with their real numerical strength.

These reasons were not enumerated to deny membership decline but point up some causal factors for the same. The fact remains that black membership is declining in the church.

The church must engage in an aggressive evangelistic program. As was stated by Bishop R. N. Brooks in the 1948 message of the College of Bishops: "Evangelism is the primary work of the Church in every age and in every land."[6] He continued:

> It is the fellowship of men and women united to Christ by a living faith, pledged to the realization of its ideals in individuals and corporate life, and committed to the great enterprise of extending His Kingdom in the World. As such, it is called to turn its attention and direct its energies to the vital work of winning people for the Master.

The recruitment of new members in the past has been too selective. Persons were sought when they were of a certain social status or occupational profile and met certain educational qualifications. Many people have lived in the primary service area of black churches but were not invited to join the Christian fellowship because they "were not our kind."

The church must seek to become an open fellowship. It must seek to recruit members without regard to race, color or economic conditions.

Parish Realignments

Black churches are often too small in membership for an adequate work load for a minister. In 1967, six out of ten charges had fewer than one hundred members. The median salary of the ministers was $1,975.00.

This had been one reason for the "moonlighting" among black ministers. To expect ministers to give full time when their salaries are below the poverty level is unreasonable indeed.

Black parishes must be enlarged. Parish development is a must for black churches. The shortage of ministerial leadership and the need to increase the workload of black ministers make it necessary to realign charges at once.

There are many types of local church cooperation. The forms most viable for black congregations are larger parishes and extended ministries. The group ministry type is the least desirable for black people. These parishes may be racial, interracial or ecumenical in composition.

The development of cooperative ministry among black churches is not an easy task. It requires patience and strenuous efforts.

Black churches have several maladies which impede the progress toward this goal. Chief among them are "stationitis" and "clositis."

147

The latter is a disease that afflicts chiefly the district superintendents. The closing of small churches has been an easy solution to the dearth of ministerial leadership. The 1948 General Conference in its action made it easy for a district superintendent to close a small church without a guilty conscience. This General Conference authorized bishops to inquire in annual conference session: How many churches have been closed this year? Their name? Their location? This was the beginning of "memorial services for dead churches."

The church should demand that a "post mortem examination" be conducted to ascertain the cause of death of these churches. Where there were many strong black churches in the past, there are now flourishing churches of other denominations or sect type today. The reason for this fact is never sought. Some black churches are submodal in a supermodal environment. Some black United Methodist Churches are dying in population areas evidencing growth.

The other disease afflicting black Methodist constituency is "stationitis," one church for the pastor only. Black ministers and black laymen are afflicted with this malady. To have a minister to serve one church is a status symbol for black laymen. Ministers, too, look upon it as the highest achievement in their ministry. It is a stepping-stone to the district superintendency. It is an exception and not the rule when a man is appointed to a district from a circuit. Because of this malady, it often has a crippling effect upon a small rural church in an extended ministry. It is often treated as a stepchild.

Since the median age of black ministers is weighted toward older men, it is difficult to establish a cooperative parish among them. When they were in seminary, they were taught to be "pastors in charge." They are not anxious to allocate responsibility now.

Another barrier to local church cooperation is the hour of worship. People have been accustomed to the "third Sunday" in each month at 11:30 o'clock. It is now sacrosanct.

It is not easy to convince people that God visits churches at other hours as well.

Church Mergers

As a last functional alternative to small churches is church merger. Precautionary measures should be taken before perfecting mergers. It should not be used as a method to develop the minimum salary for the charge. Merging churches do not always increase pastoral support. It may decrease church membership and pastoral support.

Prior to attempts to merge churches, the churches should be encouraged to engage in a creative dialogue about how they can best minister to their enlarged community. To sit together and face the problem gnawing at the heart of their community may be rewarding indeed. When people work together on some creative, mutual beneficial programs, it may lead them to desire to pool their resources. This period of experimentation may serve as a courtship period. It could lead churches to desire to become one in matrimony.

The Ministry of Reinforcement

The United Methodist Church must initiate a genuine program of the ministry reenforcement. The church must help people to help themselves in their quest for personhood. It can best be done by serving as enablers and in the consultative and supportive role. Responsible church leaders must seek to acquaint people with viable options in order that they may make responsible decisions.

In this new relationship, it may mean that white leaders will need to assume a secondary role. Instead of assuming the role ascription of president of an organizational structure, the white leaders may now need in some cases to serve as assistant secretaries.

Regardless of the role ascription, total involvement of all people is essential in achieving an inclusive fellowship. People working together on the same level in pursuit of a common goal is one way to thaw the social iceberg in American society. There are those who advocate that white churchmen can best be involved by increasing their financial assistance to the minority groups. For some this should be the limit of their participation. This is based upon the assumption that "white people do not understand." It is the candid opinion of this writer that white people understand enough to be totally involved. It is not necessary for a medical doctor to experience the pangs accompanying the birth of a child in order to help deliver a child.

Participatory and Leadership Roles

As the church continues its pursuit toward *de facto* inclusiveness on the local level, black people must play a twofold role: participatory and leadership.

Lay members and ministers must be able to participate fully at all decision-making levels in the church. Real participation is based upon mutual respect. It should never be used as a device to manipulate people. Participants must be free to vote their earnest convictions. In his book, *God's Grace and Man's Hope,* Professor Daniel Williams emphasized that a good society must rest upon every group being able to participate with power in the decision-making process.

Blacks must participate by sharing liberally of their talents, time and gifts. Total inclusiveness demands all three. *De facto* inclusiveness will not be a bequest, it is a conquest. Blacks will never be debt free.

Significant leadership roles must be ascribed to black Methodists. Honorific positions must not be tolerated in lieu of meaningful and significant roles. Due regard must be given to leadership selection. To place a black in a leadership role simply because he or she is black and can add technicolor or because he or she is manipulable, is reprehensible today. Black leaders must be chosen because of their training, experience and Christian commitment.

When roles are ascribed to blacks, they must assume full responsibility. They must evidence their stewardship. Chronic absenteeism will only permit those who answer "present" to make decisions for you and your group.

Church Extension

The need for upgrading the physical plants among black churches is long overdue. Many churches are dysfunctional. Some were erected in the period when the use of the church was confined chiefly to Sunday. Their architectural designs bespeak a day when preaching was the only expected activity of the church. Facilities for community activities and Christian education are still not available in many of the black churches.

Before planning a church extension program for black congregations, conferences would do well to engage in adequate research. What is the population trend? Can these people be served best by a new type program rather than a new structure? These are some questions that must be answered prior to an extensive church extension program.

In many cities, the white congregations are moving out to the suburbs. They are in many cases selling their churches to black congregations.

Very often these churches are too large for black congregations. All too often in anticipation of moving, these white churches are not in good repair, therefore, a poor Negro congregation is saddled with the debt and an immediate repair job. It is an almost impossible task for the average black congregation.

A sanctuary with a large seating capacity with few members in attendance has a psychological effect upon people who may attend as possible recruits. It is very difficult to recruit new members when a church has a large debt or when a few members are in attendance. No person is willing to unite with a dying institution. Likewise, a church in dire need of repair is not attractive to new members.

The home of the parsonage family must be adequate and comfortable. Some years past, Dr. Robert Wilson reported that 37 percent of the black ministers did not live in their charge. Many did not live in their charge because there was no parsonage. In many cases, the parsonages provided were not habitable. As a result, many of the ministers in the past bought their own homes out of their modest income and commuted to their charges.

Better homes for the parsonage family may be conducive to more young couples entering the parish ministry today. Men who are nearing retirement would not be likely to sell their homes and move into the new parsonage.

Increased Pastoral Support

The average black minister in the church has lived on an income below the poverty level for most of his ministry. To compensate for inadequate salary, they have of necessity had to engage in "moonlighting."

Now, to guarantee all black ministers the minimum salary within an annual conference will not be enough to attract trained young leaders today. The church must make some conscious efforts to raise the salary of these trained men above the minimum level. Trained and competent black ministers must be provided with a salary scale commensurate with their white brethren of equal qualifications.

Open Itineracy

De facto inclusiveness will come only when the church has open itineracy. Black ministers must not be frozen into their appointments because they have no place to move to receive a salary commensurate with what they are now receiving. The genius of Methodism has been its itineracy. The United Methodist Church must strive to keep this time honored system.

Open itineracy could best start with experimental parishes. Black ministers could be assigned to white charges. Likewise, white ministers could be assigned to predominantly black congregations.

Unity Through Diversity

As the church continues its quest of inclusive fellowship, "Unity Through Diversity" must be the guiding principle. The "Procrustean Bed" concept is not practical in a church composed of multi-racial groups. The church must seek to become one through functional relationships. As each organ is significant to a healthy body, each individual with his uniqueness, each group with its peculiarities is essential for a healthy fellowship. The little church in the open country can not provide a paid soloist for its morning worship. It can sing the hymns a capella with perhaps greater zest. The Negro spirituals are integral in the black experience and are as important to black people as Charles Wesley's hymns.

In the 1948 Episcopal Address, the bishops declared:

> There are differences of opinion concerning architecture. There are differences of customs in singing. . . .There must not be an attempt to regiment the church. . . . We do not wish uniformity. We do wish unity. . . . Unity must be considered in terms of spirit rather than in terms of forms. There will be unity in essentials, diversity in non-essentials. The identities which unite are more significant than the differences that divide. There will be oneness in faith, variety in order.[7]

Black Methodists must continue to respect their African heritage as well as their Methodist heritage. They do not need to trade off their rich African heritage to prove that they

153

affirm the Methodist faith. This is no time to be a mimicry of the white Methodist Christians. Black Methodists must always remember that they have made a significant contribution to the Christian faith.

Ultimate Goal of an Inclusive Fellowship

The ultimate goal of *de facto* inclusiveness on the local church level is still in the future. The United Methodist Church must remain committed to the vision of an inclusive church in an inclusive, reconciled society.

The 1964 General Conference declared that no church could bar any person from its fellowship because of race, color, or condition. General Conference legislation will not make inclusive local churches a reality. It was a start in the right direction. Inclusiveness, however, aggressively pursued, will not be an instant magical achievement.

Inclusiveness must be a two-dimensional process. In the past, it has been a unidimensional process. Black people have been urged to close their churches and unite with the white congregation. This has been a monumental blunder. The black church is the only institution that black people can claim ownership. They have a vested interest in it. Talcott Parsons sounded a warning in this regard by stating that a group or a person should not be deprived of something in which they have ownership or vested interest unless they have secured new investment as a result.

Black churches must seek actively to recruit members of other races into their fellowship. Likewise, white churches must aggressively seek to enlist black members into their churches.

For a church to be all inclusive, it must have all people in its primary service area. Residential segregation has been a barrier to an all inclusive church. Open occupancy is necessary. If the church is expected to become an integrated society, it must work to have an integrated community. Busing will not be the answer for integrated United Methodist Church.

The perennial task of the church as the Body of Christ is to make manifest the oneness of humanity in Christ through worship, service and witness. Methodism must commit itself to this task.

Notes

Chapter I

1. *The Works of the Reverend John Wesley* (New York: J. Emory and B. Waugh), 1831, Volume IV, page 12
2. J. Robinson Gregory, *A History of Methodism* (London: Charles H. Kelley, 1911), Volume I, page 180
3. *Ibid.,* page 180
4. *Ibid.,* page 220
5. *Mid-Century Report*—Division of Home Missions of the Methodist Church, 1950, page 56
6. Abel Stevens, *History of the Methodist Episcopal Church* (Cincinnati: The Methodist Book Concern), Volume IV, page 221
7. Joseph Travis, *Autobiography of The Reverend Joseph Travis,* page 101f
8. *General Minutes of the Methodist Episcopal Church,* 1817, page 295.
9. S. A. Seaman, *Annals of New York Methodism,* page 487
10. Joseph Mitchell, *The Missionary Pioneer, John Stewart, Man of Color* (1827), page 14
11. *Ibid.,* page 31
12. *Ibid.,* page 32
13. W. C. Barclay, *Early American Methodism,* Volume II, page 15
14. I. S. Thomas (ed.) *Methodism and The Negro,* page 32
15. Joseph Mitchell, *The Missionary Pioneer* (1827), page 93
16. W. T. Watkins, *Out of Aldergate* (Nashville: Department of Education of The Board of Missions of The Methodist Episcopal Church South, 1937), page 48
17. *Ibid.,* page 49
18. W. C. Barclay, *To Reform The Nation* (New York: Board of Missions and Church Extension, 1950), page 53
19. A. B. Hyde, *The Story of Methodism* (New York: M. W. Hazen Company, 1887), pages 351–352
20. W. C. Barclay, *History of Methodist Missions* (New York: Board of Missions and Church Extension), Volume I, page 268
21. John Wesley's *Thoughts Upon Slavery,* Volume XI, page 70
22. W. E. H. Lecky, *History of England in the Eighteenth Century,* Volume III, page 102
23. J. Robinson Gregory, *A History of Methodism* (London: Charles H. Kelly, 1911), Volume I, pages 101–102

Chapter II

1. W. W. Sweet, *Methodism in American History* (New York: Methodist Book Concern, 1933), page 109
2. H. E. Luccock, *The Story of Methodism* (Nashville: The Abingdon Press, 1926), page 160
3. A. B. Hyde, *The Story of Methodism* (New York: M. W. Hazen Company, 1887), page 410
4. *Ibid.*, page 411
5. M. W. Simpson, *Encyclopedia of Methodism* (Philadelphia: Everts and Everts, 1878), page 805
6. W. W. Sweet, *Methodism in American History* (New York: Methodist Book Concern, 1933), page 231
7. *Ibid.*, page 236
8. *Ibid.*, pages 229–237
9. Alexander K. McClure, *Famous American Statesmen and Orators* (New York: F. F. Lowell Company, 1902), Volume V, page 104
10. *Journal of General Conference*, 1816, pages 170–171
11. *General Conference Journal*, 1824, Volume I, page 377
12. *Christian Advocate and Journal*, June 17, 1836, page 171
13. *Christian Advocate and Journal*, Volume X, page 171
14. W. W. Sweet, *Methodism in American History* (New York: Methodist Book Concern, 1933), page 235
15. R. M. Cameron, *Methodism and Society in Historical Perspective* (Nashville: Abingdon Press, 1961) Volume I, page 174.
16. W. C. Barclay, *Early American Methodism* (New York: Board of Missions and Church Extension, 1950) Volume II, page 107
17. *Journal of the General Conference*, 1844, pages 65–66

Chapter III

1. A. Buckley, *History of Methodism in U.S.* (New York: Charles Scribner's, 1900), page 455
2. W. D. Weatherford, *Race Relations* (New York: D. C. Heath, 1934), page 208
3. *The Southern Christian Advocate I*, 1838, page 119
4. *Minutes of the Conferences*, 1845, page 603
5. A. B. Hyde, *Story of Methodism*, (New York: M. W. Hazen Company, 1888), page 540
6. *Journal of the 1844 General Conference*, page 135
7. *Christian Advocate*, May 29, 1856, Volume XXXI, page 90
8. W. K. Anderson, *Methodism* (Nashville: Methodist Publishing House, 1942), page 244
9. *General Conference Journal*, 1860, pages 244–260

Chapter IV

1. W. W. Sweet, *Methodist Church and the Civil War* (Cincinnati: The Methodist Book Concern, 1912), page 46
2. J. H. Graham, *Mississippi Circuit Riders* (Nashville: The Parthenon Press, 1967), pages 23–24
3. *Christian Advocate*, November 8, 1864, page 356
4. *Ibid.*, page 253
5. *Ibid.*, page 263
6. *General Minutes*, 1885, page 304
7. Simpson, *Encyclopedia of Methodism*, page 283
8. *Ibid.*, page 899
9. J. H. Graham, *Mississippi Circuit Riders* (Nashville: The Parthenon Press, 1967), pages 30–32
10. *Ibid.*, pages 35–36
11. W. W. Jenkins, *Steps Along The Way* (Columbia: The Socomed Press, 1967), page 5
12. *General Minutes of the Methodist Episcopal Church*, 1867, page 258
13. Graham, *Mississippi Circuit Riders*, pages 54–55
14. *Ibid.*, page 64
15. *General Conference Journal*, 1868, page 13
16. Graham, *Mississippi Circuit Riders*, page 75
17. *General Conference Journal*, 1920, page 530
18. Simpson, *Encyclopedia of Methodism*, page 664
19. *Journal of Central Alabama Conference*, 1920, pages 48–49
20. *Journal of the Southwest Conference*, 1958, pages 115–116
21. *Journal of East Tennessee Conference*, 1960, pages 106–108
22. *Journal of the Central West Conference*, 1949, pages 123–124
23. *Journal of the Upper Mississippi Conference*, 1891, page 7
24. *Journal of the Atlanta Conference*, 1940, page 84
25. *Journal of South Florida Conference*, 1925, pages 2–3
26. *General Conference Manual and Reports*, 1884, pages 14–15
27. *Ibid.*, page 19
28. *Fifth Annual Report of The Freedmen's Aid Society*, 1782, page 6
29. Sweet, *Methodism in American History*, page 34
30. *Report of the Woman's Missionary Society for 1885*, page 46
31. J. P. Brawley, *Two Centuries of Methodist Concerns* (New York: Vantage Press). This book gives a definitive statement on all of the black colleges.
32. Jay S. Stowell, *Methodist Adventures in Negro Education* (New York: The Methodist Book Concern, 1922), page 73
33. Weatherford and Johnson, *Race Relations*, page 323

Chapter V

1. *Journal of the General Conference*, 1872, page 253
2. *Journal of the General Conference*, 1896, page 439
3. *Journal of the General Conference*, 1896, page 51
4. *Journal of the General Conference*, 1912, page 213
5. D. Shaw, *Should The Negroes Be Set Apart By Themselves* (New York: Easton and Mains, 1912), pages 48–65
6. *Journal of the Upper Mississippi Conference*, 1912, page 42
7. Graham, *The Mississippi Circuit Riders*, page 142
8. *Social Forces*, Volume 42, No. 2, December, 1963
9. Weatherford and Johnson, *Race Relations*, page 58

Chapter VI

1. *General Conference Journal*, 1920, page 271
2. *Ibid.*, pages 320, 455
3. *Ibid.*, page 408, 461
4. *Ibid.*, page 461
5. *Ibid.*, page 430
6. Graham, *Mississippi Circuit Riders*, pages 151–152
7. *Journal of the Central Alabama Conference*, 1920, page 20
8. *Ibid.*, page 23
9. *Journal of the General Conference*, 1924, page 932
10. *Journal of the General Conference*, 1936, page 271
11. W. K. Anderson (ed.) *Methodism*, 1957, page 263
12. Luccock, *Story of Methodism*, page 494
13. J. M. Moore, *The Long Road to Methodist Union* (Nashville: Abingdon-Cokesbury Press, 1943), page 198
14. *Southwestern Christian Advocate*, May 20, 1937, page 325
15. Moore, *The Long Road to Methodist Union*, pages 198–199

Chapter VII

1. *Daily Christian Advocate, Central Jurisdiction*, June 20, 1940, page 8
2. *Journal of the Central Jurisdictional Conference of the Methodist Church*, 1944, pages 52–67
3. J. P. Brawley, *Matthew Simpson Davage: Elder Statesman and Reverend Sage* (1974), page 12
4. *Journal of the 1948 General Conference*, page 852
5. R. N. Brooks, *Fishing In Trouble Waters* (1951), page 22
6. *1952 Journal of the General Conference of the Methodist Church*, page 167

7. *1956 Journal of General Conference of the Methodist Church*, page 1693
8. *The 1960 Journal of the General Conference*, page 365
9. *Journal of the General Conference of The Methodist Church*, 1960, page 323
10. *Central Jurisdiction Speaks*, 1961, pages 8–9
11. *Journal of the General Conference*, 1964, Volume I, page 194
12. *Bridges to Racial Equality in the Methodist Church*, 1964, page 4
13. *Journal of the Conference of the Methodist Church*, Volume III, page 2608
14. *Ibid.*, page 2602
15. *Journal of the General Conference of the United Methodist Church*, 1972, page 502
16. *Journal of the 1968 General Conference of the United Methodist Church*, pages 927–938

Chapter VIII

1. Hyde, *The Story of Methodism*, page 744
2. *Ibid.*, page 745
3. Brawley, *Two Centuries of Methodist Concerns*, page 473
4. *Journal of the General Conference*, 1920, page 820
5. *Ibid.*, page 365
6. *Ibid.*, page 368
7. *Journal of the General Conference*, 1936, page 271
8. *Journal of the First Central Jurisdictional Conference*, 1940, page 96
9. *Ibid.*, page 98
10. *Journal of the Central Jurisdictional Conference of The Methodist Church*, 1944, pages 77–78
11. *Ibid.*, page 81
12. *Ibid.*, page 85
13. *Journal of the Third Central Jurisdictional Conference*, 1948, page 120
14. *Journal of the Fourth Session of The Central Jurisdictional Conference*, 1952, page 89
15. *Ibid.*, page 89
16. *Journal of the Fifth Session of The Central Jurisdictional Conference*, 1956, page 111
17. *Journal of the Sixth Session of the Central Jurisdictional Conference*, 1960, page 97
18. *Ibid.*, page 97
19. *Ibid.*, page 104
20. *Journal of the Seventh Session of the Central Jurisdictional Conference*, 1964, page 77
21. *Journal of the Eighth Session of the Central Jurisdictional Conference*, 1967, page 54

161

22. *Journal of the Northeastern Jurisdictional Conference,* 1968, page 288
23. *Ibid.,* 1972, page 243
24. *Journal of the South Central Jurisdictional Conference of the United Methodist Church,* 1972, page 85
25. *Report of the Woman's Home Missionary Society,* 1902, page 176
26. Graham, *Mississippi Circuit Riders,* page 134

Chapter IX

1. J. H. Graham, *The Panorama of Methodist Missions in United States,* 1962, page 8
2. J. H. Graham, *The Development of Negro Leadership for the Christian Ministry,* 1965, page 2
3. James H. Davis, *Let's Get Acquainted,* 1965, page 36
4. *Journal of the General Conference,* 1948, pages 160–162
5. *Journal of the General Conference,* 1964, Volume I, pages 962–965
6. *Journal of the Third Central Jurisdictional Conference,* 1948, pages 62–64
7. *Journal of the 1948 General Conference of The Methodist Church,* pages 170–173

www.ingramcontent.com/pod-product-compliance
Lightning Source LLC
Chambersburg PA
CBHW020448100426
42813CB00026B/3001